NEW JAPANESE VOICES

NEW

The Best Contemporary Fiction from Japan

JAPANESE

Edited by Helen Mitsios

VOICES

Introduction by Jay McInerney

A MORGAN ENTREKIN BOOK
THE ATLANTIC MONTHLY PRESS
NEW YORK

Published simultaneously in Canada
Printed in the United States of America

Library of Congress Cataloging-in-Publication Data

New Japanese voices: the best contemporary fiction from Japan / edited by Helen Mitsios: introduction by Jay McInerney.
    Contents: A callow fellow of Jewish descent / Masahiko Shimada—On meeting my 100 percent woman one fine April morning / Haruki Murakami—Swallowtails / Shiina Makoto—God is nowhere, God is now here / Itoh Seikoh—X-rated blanket / Eimi Yamada—Yu-Hee / Yang Ji Lee—On a moonless night / Sei Takekawa—Living in a maze / Kyoji Kobayashi—The imitation of Leibniz / Genichiro Takahashi—The unsinkable Molly Brown / Tamio Kageyama—Wine / Mariko Hayashi—Kitchen / Banana Yoshimoto
    1. Japanese fiction—20th century—Translations into English.
    2. English fiction—Translations from Japanese. I. Mitsios, Helen.
    PL782.E8N49 1991   895.6'3508—dc20   90-967
        ISBN 0-87113-522-1

The Atlantic Monthly Press
19 Union Square West
New York, NY 10003

First printing

ACKNOWLEDGMENTS

I owe a huge debt of gratitude to the writers and translators whose assistance, knowledge, and kindness enabled me to complete this volume.

Contents

FOREWORD

When I first heard from professor friends that Japanese literature was dead, I was resolved to the idea of pursuing a ghost. A specious opinion had led me to believe that the generation born after World War II read (if they read at all) mostly comic books and watched TV, whereas the older generation had read novels and watched films.

I was teaching Expository Writing at New York University and occasionally slipped in a few Japanese stories, usually by Mishima or Tanizaki, with the ubiquitous Norton reader. I had discovered Japanese literature as an undergraduate at Arizona State University when my creative-writing teacher had introduced me to Mishima's *Forbidden Colors.* I superimposed the Japanese sense of *wabi* (a feeling of quiet, dignified simplicity associated with a place) on the negative space of the Arizona desert. Mishima's themes of obsession, passion, jealousy, revenge (not necessarily in that order) were the very stuff of my days and nights, and years later were compelling enough that my students responded to the stories by requesting more Japanese writing. Of course there was more—the old guard. But was there new literature? Up to this point I believed—as had, it seemed, almost everyone else in America—that postwar Japanese literature was virtually nonexistent; that only a select few—writers such as Kawabata, Mishima, Oe—appealed to an international audience and perhaps more importantly, were the only writers *worth* reading outside their country. Who were the young writers? I began to wonder. Surely,

I thought, there were stories where cherry blossoms were crushed underfoot, where people rode subways to work instead of being carried in a palanquin, where instead of committing *hara kiri,* a person just gets drunk.

Far from being dead, literature in Japan today has the hybrid vigor of the traditional and the modern. The East and West. Today ninety percent of the Japanese consider themselves middle class, and the generation born after World War II has more disposable income available and fewer hardships to face than any previous one. This generation can travel the world *or* stay home, watch TV *or* movies, read comic books *or* novels, attend rock concerts *or* opera, collect CDs *or* Chanel suits.

Masahiko Shimada comes to mind when I think of Japanese writers abroad. He was the first of the group of highly acclaimed Japanese writers that I met. We sat in an old Irish bar in the West Village where the locals cast sidelong glances at the novels he had brought with him. Shimada talked about life as a writer and the necessity to travel outside of Japan. He was wearing "Queen of Hearts," a cologne he'd purchased at the GUM department store in Moscow, where he had asked (in Russian) for their most popular fragrance. Later, at a party in New York, he pulled out a libretto for *Don Giovanni* and started singing with dramatic gesticulations as his amused guests looked on.

Shimada exemplifies the common denominator each of the young writers in this book share: an energetic originality and an unbridled interest in the world around them. The writers I've chosen for this collection are among the very best in Japan, and the stories are diversely representative of fiction that has garnered these writers recognition and in many cases the most prestigious accolades in Japanese literature: the Akutagawa-*sho* and the Naoki-*sho.* If, as William James remarked, "The spectator can never know the truth," through these stories about life in Japan today the reader can at least engage in his own speculations about verisimilitude.

INTRODUCTION
by Jay McInerney

On a visit to Paris a few years ago I asked a literary critic from *Le Monde* which new American writers were making an impression in France. After a long, thoughtful pause, he replied, "William Styron." On a more recent trip to Tokyo, a time-lagged American I met in my hotel complained, "It's not like I expected—all these skyscrapers and everything"—apparently expecting pagodas. I was reminded of both of these cultural exchanges in reading a recent article about contemporary Japanese literature; it still seems to be news to American readers that Japanese fiction is not all about cherry blossoms and dueling samurai. We have not been much aware of what the Japanese have been doing in the arts, but they have been acutely aware of us, as the following stories sometimes demonstrate.

Although Japan boasts some of the world's oldest prose fictions—most notably *The Tale of Genji*—fiction enjoyed a relatively low status through the nineteenth century, vis à vis philosophy and poetry, and often tended toward the pornographic. In the twentieth century Japanese fiction has oscillated between diverse Occidental and native literary influences. Among those writers best known to Western readers, Yasunari Kawabata, the Nobel Prize–winning author of *Snow Country,* and Junichiro Tanazaki, the author of *The Makioka Sisters,* created world-class prose literature that seems thoroughly indigenous to Japan. Yukio Mishima, Kawabata's famous disciple, owed as much to Jean Genet and Dostoevsky as to Buddhist cosmology and the medieval *Haga-*

kure. When asked which Japanese writers he read, Kobo Abe, the author of *Woman in the Dunes,* once answered "none." Kafka and Beckett are the most obvious progenitors of Abe's disorienting fictional map. Kenzaburo Oe has acknowledged his debt to such Western writers as Jean-Paul Sartre and Norman Mailer, while his contemporary Shusako Endo writes from a Christian vantage point and is inevitably compared with Graham Greene. From Mishima onward, the major novelists who came of age during and after the Second World War were all deeply stamped by Western literary, philosophical, and religious influences.

The writers represented in this collection have all grown up in the period following the American occupation. They are as likely to eat toasted white bread for breakfast as rice and miso soup; their characters are as likely to graze at McDonald's as at a noodle stand. They seem to take much of the European and American cultural landscape for granted in a way that their predecessors could not. The experience that a number of these younger writers have had translating contemporary foreign authors into Japanese has inevitably influenced their own writing. Genichiro Takahashi's loopy, postmodern "Imitation of Liebniz," a meditation on baseball and sexual dysfunction with screwball diversions into metaphysics, might almost be a story by Robert Coover.

In Tanizaki, a reference to Western music or sartorial practice is loaded with ominous implications of cultural pollution and miscegenation. In the stories by these younger writers, however, Rossini's *La Gazza Ladra* and Led Zeppelin's "Whole Lotta Lovin'" simply provide the musical background, as they might in a story by Ann Beattie. (Or, for that matter, by Martin Amis or Andrea de Carlo.) Pop cultural landmarks are much in evidence; in these stories you will find references to "The Unsinkable Molly Brown," Robert Plant, and Muddy Waters. The latest novel by Kyoji Kobayashi, *She Came in Through the Bathroom Window,* takes its title from the lyrics of a Beatles song, as does Haruki Murakami's most successful novel to date. The novels of Ryu Murakami (no relation to Haruki) absolutely throb with rock songs and American movie references. The degree to which these internationally oriented young writers draw on the lingua franca of world pop culture may, paradoxically, be due to the island sense of isolation and difference that the Japanese have always felt. One feels in much of the new Japanese fiction the poignant urge to roll over Buson and Bashō, to crash through the cultural gap with the weapons most ready-to-hand; these young writers demonstrate that Hollywood, Madison Avenue, and rock and roll have generated a global reservoir of images, icons, and modern myths.

Contemporary Japanese fiction often seems to be written expressly to refute Kipling on the question of East and West. Twains meet. Yet Mariko Hayashi's "Wine" deals specifically with the question of an enduring Japanese anxiety about Occidental influences and particularly about Western Culture with a capital *C*. Intimidated into buying an exceptionally expensive bottle of French wine while on a visit to Quebec, the narrator cannot think of anyone, including herself, who will fully appreciate the gift. She is further thwarted by the strict hierarchical rules that govern gift-giving in Japan. At the end of the story she wanders aimlessly up the Ginza in the summer heat cradling a fragile, expensive bottle of wine in her arms, feeling ridiculous, unable to assimilate either herself or this artifact from the West.

The story of a young Japanese schizophrenic who goes to Paris in search of a new personal identity, Masahiko Shimada's "A Callow Fellow of Jewish Descent" is among other things a complex meditation on the Japanese obsession with the uniqueness of their cultural and racial identity. The protagonist of Shimada's story, who resents his own genes for using him as a vehicle for their survival, wonders if he might become Jewish as he is tutored in the mysteries of Judaism by a man who turns out not to be a Jew at all. We should remember that the theme of willful self-invention, so pervasive as to be nearly generic in American fiction, is highly problematic and unsettling for the team-spirited Japanese.

If young Japanese writers are cosmopolitan in their field of reference, they exhibit, from our perspective, certain native characteristics. The majority of these stories are told in the first-person singular, reflecting the influence of the *Shishosetsu,* or ego novel, the most enduring Japanese fictional genre of the century—the confessional, naturalistic narrative in which hero and author are closely identified. Japanese fiction is traditionally less plot-driven than American fiction; many of the stories in this collection challenge our need for narrative closure.

While the settings are mainly urban, the authors often refer, if only in a wistful or ironic manner, to traditional images and symbols from nature. In Sei Takekawa's "On a Moonless Night," a young woman is impregnated by a giant bee on a Tokyo street. In Banana Yoshimoto's "Kitchen," an urban dweller who loves "the great outdoors" spends most of his time in parks. Growing up in a Tokyo neighborhood from which the parkland and greenery have almost entirely disappeared, the young boy in Shiina Makoto's story "Swallowtails" is exhilarated by the metamorphosis of his collection of caterpillars into swallowtail butterflies. The first generous impulse of his cramped and somewhat selfish childhood comes as he urges the butterflies to freedom.

Inevitably there will be elements in these stories that strike most American readers as exotic and oblique—for which we should be grateful: as cultural travelers, we might hope to find at our destination something more interesting than the literary equivalents of Hilton Hotels and Holiday Inns.

A CALLOW FELLOW OF JEWISH DESCENT

Masahiko Shimada

MASAHIKO SHIMADA WAS BORN IN TOKYO IN 1961 AND GRAD-
UATED FROM THE TOKYO UNIVERSITY OF FOREIGN STUDIES.
HIS FIRST NOVEL, **YASASHII SAYOKU NO TAME NO KIYUUK-
YOKU (A DIVERTIMENTO FOR A GENTLE LEFTIST)**, WRITTEN
WHILE HE WAS A STUDENT, WAS NOMINATED FOR THE AKU-
TAGAWA AWARD; AND **MUYUU Ō-KOKU NO TAME NO ONGAKU
(MUSIC FOR A SOMNAMBULIST KINGDOM)** WON THE NOMA
LITERARY AWARD FOR NEW WRITERS IN 1984. SHIMADA'S
OTHER WORKS INCLUDE **TENGOKU GA FUTTE KURU (HEAVEN
IS FALLING DOWN)**, **NINSHIKI MASHIN ENO REKUIEMU (RE-
QUIEM FOR THE RECOGNITION MACHINE)**, **BŌMEI RYOKŌSHA
WA SAKEBI TSUBUYAKU (A REFUGEE TRAVELER CRIES AND
MUTTERS)**, **BOKU WA MOZO NINGEN (I AM A CYBORG)**,
DONNA ANNA (THIS OR THAT), AND **ARUMAJIRO-Ō (KING OF
THE ARMADILLOS)**. HIS FAVORITE AUTHORS INCLUDE GOM-
BROVICH AND KUNDERA.

1

Perhaps because the first time I visited its psychiatry department to get myself examined I asked a nurse, "Do you have a pro-
essor of philosophy here?" I was stuck with the appellation

"Tecchan"* at the hospital. Later, following my parents' strong wishes and my older brother's urgings, I went to Paris to study, where by chance I met Mr. Ludwig Penman, a Jewish Pole, and in introducing myself to him I said:

Enchanté. Je m'appelle Théchien.

I spent my one year in Paris as Théchien. During that period I rented a room in Mr. Penman's apartment and in time ended up forming something like a master-disciple relationship with him. Come to think of it now, he was the most outstanding engineer who improved my distorted thinking circuit more freely, more actively, than anyone else.

2

A small office called Refugee Stability was located above a pornographic movie theater called Film X in a corner of the Rue St. Denis. My brother worked there. Mr. Penman was the boss of that office. He used to work for a "migration agency" which helped prepare necessary paperwork for Jewish refugees from the Soviet Union and Eastern Europe and for Jewish residents in France who wanted to emigrate to Israel and other countries. But three years earlier he had become independent and expanded his business to handle not only Jews but refugees and those who wished to emigrate in general, regardless of race, providing guidance to such people as best he could. In short, he became a jack-of-all-trades in matters related to national borders. My brother was in charge of Japanese and Americans.

In fact, Refugee Stability was an exaggerated appellation, for the office rarely took up political matters. Still, Mr. Penman had done some things he could be proud of: he had helped an Armenian cellist defect; arranged to have a Turkish weight-lifter of

*Any personal name that starts with "Tetsu" tends to take the diminutive form of "Tecchan." The narrator's confused query about a "tetsguaku no sensei" (professor of philosophy) at a psychiatric department prompted the nurse to play with this custom.

A Callow Fellow of Jewish Descent

Bulgarian nationality—a candidate for an Olympic gold medal—emigrate to Turkey; undertaken the work to deposit some of the Philippine President Marcos's secret assets in an underground bank in Switzerland; and so forth. On his part, my brother did practically nothing but coordinate news coverage for Japanese TV stations and work as a tourist guide. His habitual complaint was that there was nothing as remote to the Japanese as refugees. He was not so busy as to need my help. As a result, I was shunted off to play the role of errand boy for Mr. Penman.

If I'd gone as far as Paris to train as an errand boy, I'd have to say I was being extravagant. The main purpose of my sojourn in Paris, though, was to treat my illness. Furthermore, that purpose was not my own but my parents'. No, come to think of it now, it was *their* conspiracy to kick a gloomy eccentric out of their home. My brother had written letters saying things like, "In Paris there's a gentle-hearted madame psychoanalyst called Christva. She's an old friend of Mr. Penman's, and he would be glad to introduce you to her. I envy you being examined by Christva. I ought to get ill, too." But whenever I tried to remind him of this, he'd look away and say something like, "Not many people may know this, but Mr. Penman is quite a distinguished doctor who developed an 'errand-boy treatment' for schizophrenics."

For the first half of my year, my life was like the Great Depression after 1929. Just by reminding myself of that period I can torture myself. My head was a balloon packed full of broken plates and bowls. Each time I pulsated or breathed, those broken pieces crashed into each other, almost exploding the balloon. My nerves and blood vessels were innumerable strings crazily out of tune, and each time I opened my mouth to say something, each time I took a step to walk, they resonated unbearable discordant sounds throughout my body. And my immune system was tattered, exhausted by its fight against invading germs and viruses. My body was full of holes like a box to keep insects in, and I felt coming in through those holes destructive, impulsive exhaust

gases that tempted me to suicide or crime, or else smells of gar-
lic, dust, and other particles. Total disorder! It seemed almost
impossible to reassemble me, a jigsaw puzzle, into orderly shape.
At any rate, I was hard pressed to shut off traffic with the outside
world temporarily, to prevent myself from falling apart further.

What was I so afraid of? Now I can tell you: I was certain that
I'd die soon. I was held by the illusion—it was more of a convic-
tion—that something lurked in my body that was secretly plot-
ting to drive me out of myself. What kind of basis was there for
this? There was nothing like a basis. Suppose I was taking a walk
in the Bois de Boulogne one late autumn afternoon and saw,
about sixty feet away, a prostitute in a fur coat open her chest like
a triptych, shaking out her breasts that tended to look away from
each other. What was projected on the screen at my nerve center
the next instant was not my genitals in her mouth, but my head
hanging from a branch of a beautifully shaped tree. Or I would
take a walk along the Rue St. Denis in the evening. Gradually my
walk would slow down. This was because my consciousness and
my body would slip away from each other. My consciousness
would fall one step behind my body no matter how I tried, so
that unless I stopped and corrected the slippage, I would not be
able to take the next step ahead.

I better stop. Once I begin to talk about something like this, I
can go on and on. In a healthy person's eyes my experience is
like some bait for existentialism, and it is likely to be judged that
the culprit for creating such illusions as I had was excessive self-
defense.

At least until then my life had been a series of countless negative reactions. It wasn't only that I was constitutionally prone to
food poisoning, that I was allergic to cedar pollen, or that I had
weak resistance to pathogens. It had more profound meanings.
In a word, I had inferior genes. However, I don't want to align
myself with the view that genes are what makes an individual an
individual. In defiance of that theory, I would assert:

A Callow Fellow of Jewish Descent

"The genes are thinking only of themselves. My genes and myself have nothing to do with each other. My genes are using me, a machine, for their own survival. The moment they give up on me, I'll be a heap of scrap. That's why I'm keeping company with my genes, though very reluctantly. Besides, I have to protect them from germs and viruses. They're so *delicate,* compared with other superior genes, that they force me to have a negative reaction at the drop of a hat. It makes me mad to think they'll drive me like a slave until I die. It makes me madder to think they are my parents' genes synthesized."

The doctor who examined me two weeks before I left for Paris told my parents:

"As a patient, he attacks with considerable logic. He seems to recognize some personality in his own genes. He himself has a complex dual personality. His body is pushed around by what he thinks. This is a symptom common to schizophrenics. He doesn't have to be hospitalized yet, although he'll be welcome if you want him to be. But I'd suggest you let him travel before that. He needs to learn to turn his attention outside himself. If you let him travel, though, he'd better have someone to protect him."

I had realized that I was a little ill. I didn't dislike regularly visiting the psychiatry department. The place had an inexplicable restfulness and was excellent for doing things like reading. Among its patients was a beautiful woman of noble bearing; beside her practically all the nurses looked dingy. The most annoying thing was the male nurses. They were discriminators who secured their pride in one point: they were not patients. Following Dante's classification, they'd have to live in Subdivision One, in Division Seven. That's where those who used violence against others and their possessions abide.

Fortunately, I merely wandered in the dark wood between Hell and Purgatory, and didn't have to become a settler in Hell. Incidentally, I learned about Christianity through Nietzche's writings. "Everyone has to go through a period when the outside world looks like a jungle inhabited by wild beasts," Mr. Penman once said to me. For me, who spent that particular period in Paris, Mr. Penman merged with Virgil, while my brother and parents, who enjoyed the progression of my illness as a bit of a joke, became beasts. And the Frenchmen, who regard it as a virtue to remain indifferent to others, were the trees in the wood.

Unfortunately, though, Mr. Penman and I had nothing in common. The languages he used were French, Polish, and Yiddish. He could also speak Russian. I spoke Japanese, a little bit of English, and pidgin French and Russian. Since he couldn't speak English at all, it was at first as if the fabled Asian combination of enemies, the dog and the monkey, had started communicating their thoughts to each other. Worse, he avoided speaking Russian as if it was a scourge. My brother later told me that his hatred of German was greater than that of Russian. It was a small revenge on his part. It appeared that Mr. Penman had suffered from both the Nazi persecution of Jews and imprisonment in concentration camps by the Russian SMERSH ("Death to the Spies") squad. He himself didn't say much, but the few words he did utter concerning those experiences became powerful curses. Take these words:

"If I had the slightest bit of human sentiment left in me, I wouldn't waste it in the form of love of fatherland, peace, or the spirit of self-sacrifice. People say the war's over, but I myself haven't signed any peace treaty with anybody. Has the Great Purge passed? Does that mean that I, who have survived it, am a remnant of the past? Fortunately, I left all my human sentiments in the concentration camps, so I can remain unconcerned about love of fatherland, morals, and faiths advocated by the peoples of the world as they wrangle with one another in friendly fashion."

I didn't know how to respond to someone with that kind of past, but as a matter of minimal courtesy, I put on a deferential expression when I heard such talk. I heard him through my brother's interpretation. When my brother wasn't around, I became exhausted by worries that Mr. Penman must find my presence unpleasant since I kept speaking pidgin Russian. That was one of the causes that worsened my illness. At no other time did I want to go back to that island of lovable philistines and peasants, that country of the rising sun. I should have taken an extreme step in the opposite direction and become a right-wing punk of the kind Mr. Penman would despise. And I should have habitually mouthed such inanities as "The Kwantung Army was right!" to distract myself a bit. But a combination of errand boy and right-winger would have been too much. In this regard I was a man of common sense, and chose to learn French and acquire information about the Jewish people, while cleaning Mr. Penman's apartment and serving him tea. And my curiosity about Mr. Penman—well, I was right to place it at the center of my life. The moment I did so, he automatically became my teacher.

Mr. Penman's apartment was located north of Montmartre, near the Jules-Joffrin Station. The fifth-floor flat, facing south, had a dining room, a kitchen, and five other rooms, two of which were occupied by books. I was given the smallest room, which faced west. The combination of a bed, a shoddily made closet, and a TV set was exactly like a room in a single-star hotel. Still, since I had a TV set for my exclusive use, I could spend all night doing nothing but playing computer games, paying no attention to anybody.

I was particularly devoted to a game called 'The Divine Comedy,' which, as the name suggests, told the story of Dante's journey through Hell and Purgatory as he observed things and made inquiries until he reached the Empyrean Heaven. On his way the player must seek out the guide, Virgil, or Beatrice, for advice in order to move up to the next stage. To climb up to the Empyrean Heaven, he must solve the riddles, get out of the labyrinth, and shake off those who cling to Dante's feet at each of the twenty-eight stages, thereby getting the specified number of points (called "sophia values"). To conquer the game, a player needs at least half a year, even spending two hours a day. As a result, the

conquest of the game, like my curiosity about Mr. Penman, became a daily part of my life in Paris.

I don't remember when, but just about the time I got out of
the body of Lucifer, who has three faces and six wings, and
cleared Hell, Mr. Penman came into my room and asked me to
let him play the game, too. He had secretly peeped into my room
and seen me concentrating on it late at night. I took that as proof
that he himself was curious about me, and grateful as I was for
his act of peeping, I immediately translated the instruction man-
ual of the game into French and taught him how to play it, step
by careful step.

Nevertheless, Mr. Penman gave up playing at the entrance to
Hell, in front of the River Acheron. His excuse was too severe for
a mere game:

"If you call Jesus God, you must also call Marx and Freud Gods.
I can't get myself to like the hierarchical structure of 'The Divine
Comedy.' It's the same as a bureaucracy, isn't it? I'd stick to the
earth and aim for a desert. What is there in the Heavens? The air
gets thinner, that's all."

After my brother's interpretation, I took this to be a high-class
joke and laughed, though it wasn't funny. With a stony expression
that reminded me of the Ayatollah Khomeini, Mr. Penman continued:

"I shouldn't imagine, Théchien, that for some reason you think
that life is a game, should I? A game surely has rules. But the rules
of life aren't simple enough to be understood by a single human
being. If you're planning to live your life as if its rules were the
same as the game's, you'll remain a spoiled kid forever."

My brother asked, "What in the world have you done?" I had
no choice but to turn myself into a single question mark and
attach myself right behind the word "Jew": Jew?

Mr. Penman was never a crass, hysterical scholar. Rather, your
impression was of a likable old bartender. He knew the name
and the face of the guard at the opera house, and he even knew

the backgrounds of the family who ran the store where I often went to buy fruit. I think he had acquired a special skill that couldn't be born of mere affability. It may have come from his profession. After all, an intermediary for refugees must be prepared to become a refugee himself at any time. A refugee, for the time being, has no choice but to support himself on a few things that are common to all countries, my brother said to me once. The observation must have been handed down to me straight from Mr. Penman, but it was persuasive. Among such common traits are affability, a quick sixth sense, a presentable body, aggressiveness, stamina, a driver's license—and, if I may add one more, being Jewish. Excepting the third trait, Mr. Penman met all the conditions. And having noted this, I must note I have none of them.

3

Half a year passed. Perhaps because the physical relationship between Paris and me became intimate, my negativism entered a period of lull. Then, a month later, by early March, I was free from the voodoolike thinking involving my genes. I had defeated my genes' despotic government, quelled the civil war at my nerve center, restored order, and successfully established a republic. Come to think of it now, I had been preoccupied with an utterly illogical persecution mania. In short, all I had been trying to do was to stubbornly protect my thinking circuit in its isolation.

My recovery from the illness fell on me just like a revelation. It was about the same time I conquered the game, "The Divine Comedy." The game was good for the rehabilitation of someone with schizophrenic tendencies.

As I entered the Heavenly Realm, I must have gotten what might be called a "player's high," and cleared one saint's test after another, climbed to the Ninth Heaven in three weeks, and met the Choir of Angels. I've heard that in this game it becomes difficult to get ahead once the player enters the Heavens, and that usually more than half the players give up after entering this realm. They never see what the Empyrean Heaven looks like. Beginning in the Sixth Heaven, you are given quite abstruse riddles by saints, angels, and Beatrice. At times you must have knowledge of astronomy, the basics of physics, and even a fair grasp of the history of Christianity. Besides, you aren't given optional answers, but are required to type up your own arguments in a hundred words or so. Each time this happened, I tirelessly checked the Larousse Encyclopedia (which was in Mr. Penman's library), translated the needed information into Japanese, and input it. As a result, my name was registered in the Empyrean Heaven. My intoxication at the time I finally entered it . . . I'd like to remember it as often as I can. After all, I had spent half a year just to find out how the images of the Empyrean Heaven might be displayed.

The Tenth Heaven I entered, guided by Beatrice, was so dazzling that I had to put on a pair of sunglasses. There it was no longer necessary to punch the keyboard. All I had to do was to stare at the images given as beneficences. The pleasure of stoicism brought on not by a drug but by an endurance lasting for half a year . . . at that moment my brain was as lucid as the night above a desert where countless stars flash. Beatrice, wearing only a robe of light, held out her hands. Around her were angels dancing wildly in a weaving motion like that of a roller coaster running on loops. They played the Paradise Song in Fauré's *Requiem*. Now one with Dante, I flitted like a butterfly from one pistil of white roses to another. There I saw the dear women I met in Purgatory, Rachel and Eudit. Next I met the Virgin Mary. A close-up of her face. Looking exactly like the picture of the Virgin Mary that Raphael is said to have painted with a baker's daughter as his model, she winked. The next moment Dante = I, along with Beatrice, was sucked into the Virgin Mary's crotch. Then began a memoir of Hell and Purgatory. The records of the journey, which took a total of three hundred hours, floated up one after another in flashes. Devils with rakes, usurers, snakes, jolly robbers, our friend Caserla who sang love songs for us, souls like invisible men praying in tears. . . . Soon all of them showed up en masse on the screen and, bumping and falling, gradually turned into brilliantly colored marble patterns. Dante = I merged with Beatrice and melted into them.

These images were made to last forever and did not stop unless you turned the power off. For fully two hours I continued to watch them. If you punched the keyboard, the marble patterns changed into various shapes. Depending on what you thought, they looked like a nebula, a carnival scene, or an ugly monster. Sometimes a sexy Virgin Mary or a Beatrice with a funny face showed up; or all the patterns disappeared and something like a full moon casting pale blue light appeared; or the whole thing turned into purling electric waves like those you see after broadcasting on TV is over.

I saw God in the disorder.

Is it an exaggeration to say this? At least, I am certain that I thought a God with some shape or figure was cheap. The Jewish God is expressed with the four letters, Y, H, W, and H, but according to one of the ten commandments you can't chant "Yahweh" in vain, and you aren't allowed to make any image of him. In this regard I easily sympathize with the followers of Judaism who have no idols or icons, although I must say that my God is spelled WXY, which represents the female body, and is pronounced, "Gee, it stinks!" In telling Mr. Penman that I had conquered the game "The Divine Comedy," I said something like this:

"I thought that God and nature, God and disorder, were the same. God must be what is nothing and everything."

Mr. Penman showed a flicker of interest and said:

"In my boyhood I was taught that by a rabbi. Yes, from my childhood I thought it silly to revere Jesus as God. Seeing Jews insisting on The Law and trying to make its interpretations ever more complicated, that fellow made fun of them. This happened to please the dumb people. In personality Jesus was a man like

Marx, Freud, or Einstein. Your game is made better than the original version of *The Divine Comedy*, if it educated you in such a way as to make you feel that."

"Monsieur Penman, does that mean Jesus criticized the followers of Judaism just as Nietzsche did Christians?"

"Well, that wasn't exactly the case, but you're more or less right. In the first place, Jesus had nothing to do with Christianity. He was no more than a man with a special constitution capable of wandering in a desert. Of course, he was smart and was of the sort that attracted people's interest. Just think. Which will people prefer—a scholar who sweats over the interpretation of each and every word and phrase of The Law, or a fellow who sums up in a word what's written in The Law? Those bastards who wrote the New Testament are to blame for everything."

Attracted by the way he said these things, I studied French with an intensity I hadn't had since the entrance examinations.

4

In April, in addition to the conquest of the game "The Divine Comedy," there was another event that made my health take a turn for the better: a vacation in Southern France. I managed sightseeing for the first time in my seventh month in France. There was no better rehabilitation than a ten-day tour of Nice, St. Paul, and Monaco. From the food on the plane, an airport bar, and a salon car made by Renault, to the curtains in a hotel room—everything made me lightheaded with the joy of discovering values that were plainly visible but not noticed till then. Does the strong sunlight give an aura to ordinary things? Quite aside from this, what this city mouse felt in visiting resort places was that most of the people there were children.

We—the five of us, that is: Mr. Penman; my brother; my brother's lover, Claudine; Mr. Penman's secretary, Marusha; and I—did things together during the day and separately during the night. My brother and Clau (he called her that) disappeared every other night, but the rest of us stayed in the mansion owned by Mr. Penman's friend (who was absent). In Nice, too, I was still an errand boy, and every morning I went out by bicycle to fetch croissants and whatever was needed for lunch that day. In cooking I offered almost all the ideas and skills, and the four others puttered about only when dishing things out. I made bouillabaisse and roasted fowl and, when so inclined, served thinly cut slices of raw flounder. Everyone recognized my talent as a cook.

Once, at Mr. Penman's request, I prepared a dinner consisting only of fried eggs, bread, and salad of green vegetables. It was the first night of Pesach. It appeared that the vacation had been planned to fall on Pesach. But with four heathens this Pesach ended up as a party to console Mr. Penman for his solitude.

"In the old days all the relatives used to get together and make a big celebration of it," Mr. Penman sighed as he rarely did. "Whenever this time of the year comes around, I regret I didn't have any children."

"How about adopting my brother?" said my brother in an insensitively jolly voice. "He tells me he'd like to prostrate himself before Judaism. He also respects you, Monsieur Penman."

Ever sensitive to French spoken with a Japanese accent, I bluntly expressed my view, "I don't like Judaism."

"I don't like it, either," Mr. Penman sneered with his nose, without changing his Ayatollah Khomeini expression. "If an anti-Semite riot took place in my heart, that would be because of the hard-headed followers of Judaism. Wherever I may be, I remain a Jew, but before that I'm a stranger. Just as Christ and Marx were strangers to their contemporary Jews."

"In my heart there's an anti-Japanese riot constantly," I said, borrowing Mr. Penman's expression. "At the same time, somewhere in my heart, I am an imperialist. I'd like to be freed from this aspect of being Japanese."

Mr. Penman suddenly exploded a husky laugh. "Théchien, you are some pacifist. Unfortunately, though, a half-hearted human being like you won't be taken seriously in any place. The best you can do is to try not to give unpleasant impressions to people, but to try to be loved. Neutralistic people arouse the most suspicion. Every human being alive in this world is somebody. For example, suppose you go to Israel and ask to be made a Jew. They'll tell you, first have a self-awareness as a Japanese. Only then can we become friends."

"But for the Jews," Claudine interjected, "heathen friends are also enemies, aren't they?" My brother put his mouth close to her ear and said, "Stop that."

"Discriminators are common to all countries. They are among the Jews and the French—though, if anything, there may be more of them among the French."

"I don't think it's a question of number. Everybody has a sense of discrimination, more or less. I find weird the notion that everybody should be friendly and equal. I prefer French women to Italian women. Japanese women are inferior to Chinese women. That's because in Japan there are few hybrids."

My brother had an absolutely low opinion of the Japanese. He hadn't come out of the Francomania of his student days, and as a seven-year settler in Paris, he affected the airs of a refugee. Still, his thinking wasn't too different from that of a Japanese "salaried man," for he said to me from time to time that he'd like to buy a good co-op within thirty minutes of commuting distance and settle down with Clau as soon as he could. Claudine was a clerk at the Museum of African and Oceanic Art. Intellectually Italian, sexually French—"If the reverse were the case, I'd have no complaint," my brother secretly grumbled, making me suspect that their marriage wouldn't go too well.

In the end, the four of us, excluding Mr. Penman, each came up with his own reason for celebration to keep Mr. Penman's company at Pesach. I celebrated the recovery from my illness, my brother counted the days since he met Clau and celebrated the

A Callow Fellow of Jewish Descent

481st day since their encounter, and Marusha, the secretary, celebrated the health of her Polish father, who had defected.

We enjoyed cruising on the third and fourth day of our vacation, and on the fifth we went to the village of St. Paul. There we drank champagne watching Yves Montand playing *pétanque* with a large bet, and went to see a famous astrologer to have him tell us about our futures. It appeared that I was to encounter in the near future a big incident which might greatly change my life. When I asked whether the incident was going to be good or bad for me, I was told, "If you get deeper into it, you might run into some danger, but it's going to be good on the whole." As for Mr. Penman, he was told, "If you pay attention to your health and value your friends, you can get through the year without any problem. Two years from now, the inclination of your star will improve."

During the second half of our vacation, my brother and Clau disappeared, Marusha went to visit a friend, and Mr. Penman and I frequented a casino in Monaco. To return to Japan I had to make enough money for the airfare on my own, but the wage Mr. Penman's company paid me was 1,500 francs (less than ¥40,000) a month, not much more than a student loan. Unless I hit the jackpot at a casino, I would be forced to stay in Paris another six months.

However, whereas a casino is gentle to those who mean to play with coincidences in a healthy fashion, and gives some aid to those who attempt to find some inevitability in coincidences, it remains absolutely cold to those with a greedy bent who'd rush to a gold mine if they heard of one. I clung to roulette for five hours and lost 2,000 francs. Mr. Penman, who's shrewd in everything, continued to bet on zero for an hour and, when he happened to bet 1,000 francs, he won and triumphantly left, after giving me and the dealer 500 francs each.

On the last night of our vacation, Mr. Penman invited the four of us to a restaurant at the top of Ez. Ez is known to be the place where Nietzsche thought up and penned *Thus Spake Zarathu-stra*. Because there also was "Nietzsche's promenade," I offered this impression:

"The mountain where Zarathustra is said to have shut himself up may turn out to be as resorty as this, and when he got tired of writing, he may occasionally have come down to eat some tortoise soup, don't you think?"

Mr. Penman sniffed as usual and said: "There are no books on mountains and in deserts, are there? That's what's important. How to read nature and one's own body—that is the basis of philosophy. In this regard ancient Greeks were healthy. In contrast, we Jews have been unhealthy since the olden days. You see, even our daily life is tightly bound up by the Bible, Talmud, and Halakah. The body of a Jew is fettered with words. When you think of it, it may be we Jews who need a philosopher like Nietzsche—though he's German, and no Jew would read him seriously."

My brother, who showed great reluctance to serve as an interpreter, pleaded, "Would you refrain from talking any more about such complicated things?" But by then I could understand most of what Mr. Penman said without interpretation.

I suspect that Mr. Penman recognized me as his disciple and felt joy in imbuing me with his thoughts. The vacation in Southern France was meant to be a lesson to restore my consciousness to my body, as well as a stage for Mr. Penman to talk about his philosophy.

5

After returning to Paris I offered to translate Mr. Penman's writings into Japanese. I explained that, having conquered "The Divine Comedy," I wanted to have some work for times when I had nothing to do. His response wasn't too good, however.

"A publisher has been found for the records of the work we've done at Refugee Stability. But your brother is doing the translation into Japanese. I published my writings in the past, but for my own reasons I destroyed all of them. I'm writing a memoir now. When I've completed it, I'll give you a copy, too."

So I began to read some of the more notable titles I found in Mr. Penman's library, but I gave up on every one of them and left them unfinished. This was because as Japan's "Golden Week"* arrived I was forced to work as a guide for hordes of tourists from Japan. I received training under my brother for only three days and rushed tourist groups around the Louvre, Montmartre, the Pompidou Center, and the Garden of the Tuileries. This work gave me a good opportunity to sightsee Paris in a serious fashion. Pressed by the necessity, I learned to speak freely the kind of French needed for conducting daily business. When one of the tourists asked me to introduce him to a prostitute without AIDS, I gave him the telephone number of my brother's apartment, saying that he was a pimp specializing in Japanese.

While my brother and I were kept extremely busy with the guide work, Mr. Penman was working on two cases. One of them had to do with his acting as an agent for a French-Africaner family of the Republic of South Africa who'd decided to live in Paris. The other was finding work for an immigrant worker fresh from Portugal. When I asked him about the details of the work involved in these cases, Mr. Penman said, "So you want to steal the know-how of my work?" But he then followed the remark with a vivid explanation of the negotiations at the Immigration Office of the Ministry of Foreign Affairs and how to concoct the positions and arguments best suited for immigration. I was interested in the fees he would get, but he didn't give precise answers, making me guess the amounts by saying, "My fees are such that they don't make the defectors feel gratitude to me, but they don't make them hate me, either."

Until June the tour-guide work kept me busy; as a result, I was

*A week from the end of April to early May when national holidays occur every other day.

able to build a windfall fortune (though the amount was about the same as what Mr. Penman made at the casino). That was enough for me to get out of Paris. When I thought hard about it, though, I had by then acquired more detailed knowledge about the geography of Paris than that of Tokyo, and from the viewpoint of my closeness to my teacher and the range of friends and acquaintances I'd developed, it was more advantageous to stay on in Paris. My life in Tokyo was quite sequestered, as it was limited to my apartment, the hospital, and about three friends.

But the moment I decided to stay on in Paris for one more year or so, my brother meddled. For a long time he'd had the bad habit of using his younger brother like a possession of his own.

"You've cured your illness by coming to Paris, haven't you? I wouldn't say that was thanks to me, but you would give me some credit, too, wouldn't you? I have a special favor to ask. Will you do it for me?"

I said, "No," in anticipation of what was to come.

"Hey, I haven't said anything yet. It's a simple thing. All you do is go back to Tokyo. All I ask you to do is something you can do in two hours. I've decided to marry Clau. We'll have a wedding here in August. When I told this to Mom, she began to insist that we have the wedding ceremony in Tokyo. But Clau's parents are stubborn, too. They say lovers in Paris ought to live in Paris and get married in Paris. To get out of this bind, we've decided to go to Japan on a honeymoon around September and, to convince Mom, to have a wedding ceremony in Tokyo, too. Then we'll return to France on another honeymoon. An excellent plan, isn't it? So, I'd like you to return to Tokyo ahead of me and pick the places for the wedding and the party that follows, and make other arrangements. You mail the invitations, too. You'll do that, won't you? If you don't, I'll be in trouble. There are things you've got to do, like making reservations and figuring out the costs. Unless I'm nice to Pop and Mom, I can't expect them to give me any financial aid."

He tried to persuade me twice, three times. Finally I had to agree, though on condition that he give me round-trip airfare. When I told this to Mr. Penman, he sneered through his nose three times (unlike the usual two) and muttered—I couldn't tell whether it was a monologue or he was talking to me:

"A round-trip means you plan to come back here. You better live wherever you want to. There's no reason you shouldn't use that freedom."

After a while he asked how old I was. When he learned I was twenty-five, he did some counting on his fingers.

"You could have been my child when I was forty-one," he said. "You're still young. You can still become anything. I can't be any other thing than a Jew. It's too late now. The next time I'm re-born, I'd like to be Japanese."

Mr. Penman sank deeply into his sofa and turned his attention to the portrait of some rabbi hung on the wall.

6

On the day I left Paris, Mr. Penman handed me an envelope, telling me to translate it on the plane. Written in it were words of blessing that also whipped me.

To My Dear Son, Théchicn,

You don't seem to have any consciousness other than cu-riosity. One can draw your portrait by simply rubbing this morning's newspaper on a pure-white wall. Faded stains of ink—that is all of you. There's nothing else. You are wonder-fully zero. I envy you so. After all, you can always begin from zero. Yes, if equipped with curiosity, you can discard con-ventional morality, jealousies, and vengeful sentiments for something, simple comedies and faith in wooden idols, let alone joys, angers, sorrows, and pleasures that merely scatter noises about. There's nothing to worry. They are like germs and parasites, sometimes making human beings ferment, sometimes making them rot. Usually we evaluate a human being by the degree of his fermentation or rotting and judge who he is. But you are an exception. Because curiosity constantly pulls you outside yourself, you can't become anybody forever. The only certain thing is that you have a special constitution whose identity can't be ascertained. A single mistake, and you'll be an idiot; at best, a callow fellow or a bankrupt personality. You can continue to live only by getting food through other people's compassion or by being treated nicely by some teacher who's eager to teach you personal virtues, morality, and how to make it in the world. Fortunately, you are no fool. If things work out, you may become a man surpassing human beings. Don't misunderstand. By "a man surpassing human beings," mind you, I don't mean a superman. All I mean is that your special constitution can't be understood by a traditional view of human beings. If you have value beyond that, make it on your own as you like.

Your old disciple,

LUDWIG PENMAN

I wanted to think that this letter expressed the essence of Mr. Penman's thought. With the specimen called Théchien before him, he must have wondered how to explain it. Just as Mr. Penman was a stranger to me, I must have been the Sphinx's riddle to him. No game requires you more to use your head than an encounter with something whose identity can't be explained. In this regard, my encounter with him was a philosophical event.

At each person's nerve center swirls his own thinking circuit. The swirl is generated by group environments such as society, race, and nation, and the power relations among the morals, disciplines, education, and laws that are forced upon them; it is then individualized through the complex layering of information and knowledge that pours into it through mass media. A true teacher must be someone who pulls out to an airy spot the thinking circuit that tends to burrow into someplace closed. At the same time he must be someone who can distinguish things that are common to his own in his disciple's thinking circuit from things that are different from his.

In my true teacher Mr. Penman's letter, I sensed even a touch of jealousy for my youth, my half-heartedness, and my nonpersonality. I continued to marvel at the wonderful way he'd aged.

7

When I had finished the chores my brother asked me to do and was planning the time to return to Paris, I had a telephone call from my brother. He liked to throw out conventional jokes in serious guises. But this time he didn't sound like his usual self in reporting an incident: "Monsieur Penman was beaten up by a young Jew and has ended up in a hospital!"

He continued, crushing any opportunity for me to ask a question.

"I learned about the circumstances from the police today. It appears that Monsieur Penman is no Jew. That his youth was ruined by the Nazis and that he missed the chance to live his youth because of his imprisonment in Russian concentration camps were both lies, it seems. What are you going to do? He was from a bourgeois Polish family, and in the confusion right after the war decided to pretend to be Jewish. 'Shit, how can a fellow who isn't a Jew pretend to be one?' thought some poor Zionist of the religious sect who got hold of the information, it seems, and he resorted to a radical measure."

"Is Mr. Penman all right?"

"I hear he broke his collarbone. But he can leave the hospital in a week. I can't tell you how busy I am."

"Listen, is it a fact that Mr. Penman isn't a Jew? I can't believe it."

"You may believe it. Penman himself has confessed it. 'I'm not a Jew, but have become one by making efforts,' is what he said.

In his business he can make more money and get more work by being a Jew than by being a Pole. Jews are said to be good businessmen, but Monsieur Penman, who took advantage of that, is an actor one cut above. Are you shocked?"

I think I was considerably shocked, for I suffered acute aphasia.

"But he's great, don't you think? To become Jewish he must have spent a considerable amount of time studying Yiddish and various customs. He may have been in Israel as a French spy. If he was, his current business must be a cinch for him. But the world is complicated, isn't it? There are a disgusting number of things *you* can't understand with your head. By the way, about our wedding in Tokyo, I heard you worked out everything all right. You saved me. At this end it's business as usual. Whether Monsieur Penman is Jewish or Polish has nothing to do with us for now. Everything will remain unchanged, as it has been. Look, we'll see you in Tokyo in September. Stay well. Write a letter to Monsieur Penman."

My humble Shangri-La illuminated by the Mediterranean sun and the dazzling light of the Empyrean Heaven was now surrounded by a desert. In this desert that suddenly opened up before my eyes lived Mr. Penman. Surely a resident of the same Shangri-La with me until yesterday, he had now left for the desert with new riddles.

I hesitated to step into this desert. Could I possibly bear the hell of translating myself into a Jew? At least at that moment I didn't want to think about anything like that.

Translated by Hiroaki Sato

ON MEETING MY 100 PERCENT WOMAN ONE FINE APRIL MORNING

Haruki Murakami

BORN IN KOBE IN 1949, HARUKI MURAKAMI STUDIED AT WA-
SEDA UNIVERSITY, THEN MANAGED A JAZZ BAR IN TOKYO
FROM 1974 TO 1981. HE RECEIVED THE NOMA LITERARY
AWARD FOR NEW WRITERS FOR HIS NOVEL **A WILD SHEEP
CHASE**. **THE END OF THE WORLD** AND **THE HARD-BOILED
WONDERLAND** WERE AWARDED THE TANIZAKI PRIZE. HIS
NORWEGIAN WOOD SOLD MORE THAN FOUR MILLION COP-
IES, AND **DANCE, DANCE, DANCE,** HIS MOST RECENT NOVEL,
HAS SOLD MORE THAN A MILLION COPIES TO DATE.

One fine April morning, I passed my 100 percent woman on a Harajuku back street.

She wasn't an especially pretty woman. It wasn't that she was wearing fine clothes, either. In the back, her hair still showed how she'd slept on it; and her age must already have been close to thirty. Nonetheless, even from fifty meters away, I knew it: she is the 100 percent woman for me. From the moment her figure caught my eye, my chest shook wildly; my mouth was parched dry as a desert.

Maybe you have a type of woman that you like. For example, you think, women with slender ankles are good; or, all in all, it's women with big eyes; or it's definitely women with pretty fingers; or, I don't understand it, but I'm attracted to women who take a lot of time to eat a meal—something like that. Of course, I have that kind of preference. I've even been distracted, eating at a restaurant, by the shape of a woman's nose at the next table.

But no one can "typify" the 100 percent woman at all.

I absolutely cannot even remember what her nose looked like—not even whether she had a nose or not, only that she wasn't especially beautiful. How bizarre!

I tell someone, "Yesterday I passed my one hundred percent woman on the street."

"Hmm," he replies, "was she a beauty?"

"No, it wasn't that."

"Oh, she was the type you like?"

"That I don't remember. What shape her eyes were or whether her breasts were big or small, I don't remember anything at all about that."

"That's strange, isn't it?"

"Really strange."

"So," he said, sounding bored, "did you do anything, speak to her, follow her, huh?"

"I didn't do anything," I said. "Only just passed her."

She was walking from east to west and I was heading west to east. It was a very happy April morning.

I think I would have liked to have a talk with her, even thirty minutes would have been fine. I would have liked to hear about her life; I would have liked to open up about mine. And, more than anything, I think I'd like to clear up the facts about the kind of fate that led us to pass on a Harajuku back street one fine morning in April 1981. No doubt there's some kind of tender secret in there, just like the ones in the souls of old-time machines.

After that talk we would have lunch somewhere, maybe see a movie, go to a hotel lounge and drink cocktails or something. If everything went well, after that I might even be able to sleep with her.

Opportunity knocks on the door of my heart.

The distance separating her and myself is already closing down to only fifteen meters.

Now, how in the world should I speak up to her?

"Good morning. Would you please speak with me for just thirty minutes?"

That's absurd. It sounds like an insurance come-on.

"Excuse me, is there a twenty-four-hour cleaning shop around here?"

This is absurd, too. First of all, I'm not carrying a laundry basket, am I? Maybe it would be best to speak out sincerely. "Good morning. You really are my one hundred percent woman."

She probably wouldn't believe that confession. Besides, even if she believed it, she might think she didn't want to talk to me at all. Even if I'm your 100 percent woman, you really are not my 100 percent man, she might say. If it should come to that, no doubt I'd just end up completely flustered. I'm already thirty-two, and when you get down to it, that's what getting older is like.

In front of a flower shop, I pass her. A slight, warm puff of air touches my skin. Water is running on the asphalt sidewalk; the smell of roses is in the air. I can't speak out to her. She is wearing a white sweater, she's carrying an envelope that isn't stamped yet in her right hand. She's written someone a letter. Since she has extremely sleepy eyes, maybe she spent all night writing it. And all of her secrets might be carried inside that envelope.

After walking on a few more steps, when I turned around, her figure had already disappeared into the crowd.

* * *

Of course, now I know exactly how I should have spoken up to her then. But, no matter what, it's such a long confession I know I wouldn't have been able to say it well. I'm always thinking of things like this that aren't realistic.

Anyway, that confession starts, "once upon a time," and ends, "isn't that a sad story?"

Once upon a time, in a certain place, there was a young boy and a young girl. The young boy was eighteen; the young girl was sixteen. He was not an especially handsome boy; she was not an especially pretty girl, either. They were an average young man and young woman, just like lonely people anywhere. But they believed firmly, without doubt, that somewhere in this world their perfect 100 percent partners really existed.

One day it happened that the two suddenly met at a street corner. "What a surprise! I've been looking for you for a long time. You might not believe this, but you are the one hundred percent woman for me," the man says to the young woman.

The young woman says to the young man, "You yourself are my one-hundred percent man, too. In every way you are what I imagined. This really seems like a dream!"

The couple sat on a park bench, and they continued talking without ever getting tired. The two were no longer lonely. How wonderful to claim a 100 percent partner and be claimed as one too!

However, a tiny, really tiny, doubt drifted across their hearts; could it really be all right for a dream to come completely true this simply?

When the conversation happened to pause, the young man spoke like this.

"Well, shall we give this another try? If we're really, truly the one hundred percent lovers for each other, surely, no doubt, we can meet again sometime, somewhere. And this next time we meet, if we're really each other's one hundred percent, then let's get married right away. OK?"

"OK," the young woman said.

And the two parted.

However, if the truth be told, it wasn't really necessary to give it another try. That's because they were really and truly the 100 percent lovers for each other. Now, it came to pass that the two were tossed about in the usual waves of fate.

One winter, the two caught a bad flu that was going around that year. After wandering on the borderline of life and death for several weeks, they ended up having quite lost their old memories. When they came to, the insides of their heads, like D. H. Lawrence's childhood savings bank, were empty.

But since the two were a wise and patient young man and young woman, piling effort upon effort, they put new knowledge and feeling into themselves again, and they were able to return to society splendidly. In fact, they even became able to do things like transfer on the subway or send a special-delivery letter at the post office. And they were even able to regain 75 percent or 85 percent of their ability to fall in love.

In that way, the young man became thirty-two, the young woman became thirty. Time went by surprisingly fast.

And one fine April morning, in order to have breakfast coffee, the young man was headed from west to east on a Harajuku back street, and in order to buy a special-delivery stamp the young woman was headed from east to west on the same street. In the middle of the block the couple passed. A weak light from their lost memories shone out for one instant in their hearts.

She is the 100 percent woman for me.

He is the 100 percent man for me.

However, the light of their memories was too weak, and their words didn't rise as they had fourteen years ago. The couple

passed without words, and they disappeared like that completely
into the crowd.

Isn't that a sad story?

That's what I should have tried to tell her.

Translated by Kevin Flanagan and Tamotsu Omi

SWALLOWTAILS

Shiina Makoto

SHIINA MAKOTO WAS BORN IN 1944 IN SETAGAYA, TOKYO. AFTER GRADUATING FROM TOKYO UNIVERSITY OF PHOTOGRAPHY, HE WORKED AS THE EDITOR OF **STORES REPORT,** A TRADE MAGAZINE, UNTIL 1976, WHEN HE STARTED **HON NO ZASSHI (THE MAGAZINE OF BOOKS)**, OF WHICH HE HAS BEEN THE EDITOR SINCE. MAKOTO'S LITERARY CAREER BEGAN IN 1979, AND HE RECEIVED THE TWENTY-THIRD YOSHIKAWA EIJI LITERARY AWARD FOR NEW WRITERS IN 1989 FOR HIS **INU NO KEIFU (THE PEDIGREE OF A DOG)**.

MAKOTO'S OTHER LITERARY WORKS INCLUDE **AISHU NO MACHI NI KIRI GA FURU NODA (A MIST FALLS ON THE TOWN OF SORROW)**, **GAKU MONOGATARI (THE TALES OF MOUNTAINS)**, **KATSUJI NO SA-KASU (CIRCUS OF PRINT TYPES)**, AND **AD BIRD**. HIS PHOTOGRAPHS INCLUDE **GOING OUT TO SEE THE SEA,** AND HAVE BEEN PUBLISHED AND EXHIBITED WIDELY.

THE AUTHOR ENJOYS REMOTE REGIONS OF THE WORLD AND HAS TRAVELED TO MORE THAN THIRTY COUNTRIES. HE HAS VISITED THE STRAIT OF MAGELLAN AND CAPE HORN, THE CENTRAL DESERT OF AUSTRALIA, AND THE SITE OF LOU-LAN, THE ANCIENT CAPITAL OF THE UIGUR DISTRICT OF CHINA. HE IS PLANNING A TRIP TO MONGOLIA.

"Hey, Dad, am I bald?" Takashi suddenly asked me one day when we were in the bath, with a serious look on his face.

"No, Takashi, you're not bald," I said. I wanted to laugh, but the expression on his face was so serious that I felt a bit unnerved.

"Oh. But Yuji and those guys keep calling me a bald-headed monk."

"Well, it's true your head is shaved, but you're not bald. Bald means you don't have any hair on your head."

"Oh, really?" Takashi thought about this. "Then I guess it was OK," he said, evidently satisfied about something.

My son had always had his head shaved. At first I used to take him with me to a barbershop whenever his hair grew long, but it got to be a pain and I thought it was silly to spend ¥1,600 to cut a head of hair as small as that. So I bought an electric hair-clipper and did the job myself. I'd take him into the bath, strip him, and shave his head. In the beginning I didn't know how hard to press or how fast to move, and Takashi would scream a lot. After three years, though, it got to the point where just shaving Takashi's head wasn't quite enough for me. So I'd shave two or three other kids' heads as well.

"What was OK?" I asked, feeling a little nervous about Takashi's sudden calmness.

"Well, Yuji kept calling me a bald-headed monk, so today I hit him." Takashi looked straight at me without a smile and then began cleaning the back of his neck with a soapy towel. I'd already heard that, apparently, my son was the only one in his class with a shaved head.

"You hit him?"

"Yep."

"What happened then?"

"Yuji started crying."

"Are you and Yuji in the same class?"

"No."

"What class, then?"

"He's a third-grader. Yuji Yoshino, third grade, first class."

"I see."

I looked at Takashi's round, clean-shaven head, which was still about another two weeks from its next shave, and said nothing.

Then I suddenly recalled the report card he brought home at the end of first grade. His grades were as bad as I thought they would be, but I wasn't prepared for what the teacher said about his behavior. Under the "Getting Along with Others" section was written this:

"For some reason, Takashi seems aggressive. When I asked his classmates if they had ever been hit by him, two thirds of them raised their hands."

My wife turned slightly pale and fell silent when she saw this. We'd never dreamed something like this was happening; it was hard to believe.

"Maybe we just didn't raise him right," she said later, whispering in the dark of a spring night so cold that it was spring in name only.

"No, I don't think it's that," I said, as cheerfully as I could. "I think what we did was fine."

The worried way in which she spoke sounded like the way people talk about how badly poor parents raise their children.

About a year before Takashi was to enter school, my wife and I talked it over and decided that we weren't going to send him to preschool.

Kodaira, an out-of-the-way town on the Musashino Plain where I live, is a classic Tokyo bedroom community. There seem to be a lot of households here with very pointed ideas on education, about which they are excessively clamorous. It is, in fact, the perfect nesting place for mothers with an obsessive concern about the education of their children. These are the mothers who in all seriousness ask kindergarten teachers such sickening questions as what they should have their children learn, absorb, understand, and otherwise master before entering school, imploring the teachers to advise them on the matter.

For better or worse, my son went to a noisy city-run nursery school locked in a battle over wages that left the staff with little time to attend to the children. From an odd sense of destiny engendered by this environment, we never gave Takashi the kind of bizarre schooling most of his peers got.

Takashi, for his part, thoroughly enjoyed himself at this nursery. He was happy to spend the entire day running wild with his friends, returning home at night to wrestle and box with his boring father.

Shortly after Takashi entered school, however, it became clear to us that children these days are thoroughly schooled in a variety of subjects at home, even before they enter school. Everyone in Takashi's class could easily read, and many could also write. Of the thirty-four pupils in my son's class, he alone could neither read nor write.

One day, two or three months after he started school, I asked Takashi if he liked it. He did; his eyes sparkled with excitement. He thought the nursery school on the whole had been more fun because he didn't have to study, but characteristically he allowed that school was better because he could play soccer.

The second semester started while my wife and I were still trying to figure out what we could or should do about the first-semester reports of our son's lawless behavior. For Takashi, as always, the best part about going to school was being able to play with his friends. But with the start of the second semester many of his friends started practicing the piano or taking English conversation classes, and there were fewer and fewer opportunities for him to play every day with a dozen or more friends until dusk and exhaustion set in.

Sadly, too, the parks and open spaces in which children could play seemed to have suddenly disappeared.

The school prohibited use of the playground there after 3:40 in the afternoon, when the gates were closed and the children sent straight home. Students couldn't use the grounds on Sundays because they were taken over by city baseball teams and soccer clubs. The reason for this was that, supposedly, the school didn't want to be held responsible for injuries incurred by students using the playground.

Croquet became the craze with old people at about this time, and what little open space existed inside the city was, by city decree, quickly turned into croquet grounds. The grounds were surrounded by barbed-wire fences—to keep the children from ruining the grounds when they weren't in use.

That day Takashi, who was lying on his bed, called me. Ever since he could talk, he's addressed his parents without using the *-san* suffix—*otou* instead of *otousan,* for example. I asked him why he never did so. He said we weren't important enough for the *-san*. That time, too, he wore an unexpectedly serious expression on his face.

"*Otou,*" he said again, "today I went to that park over there—Atchan-Yama Koen—and it'd been turned into another croquet ground. The only place left where we can play baseball is Central Park, but the adults there get angry at us right away, and nobody wants to play there anymore."

"That park has gotten to be really terrible," I said.

Central Park used to be a large testing site full of big ginkgo trees and mulberry fields. At first the city got rid of the mulberry trees and turned the area into a large grass field, which was very nice. On Sundays I would take Takashi, who was still in nursery school, to that park. It was big enough to have four grass baseball fields, and even on Sundays teams would be engaged in fierce struggles from early in the morning. Children would play baseball and soccer in the small spaces around the fields. To the people in the neighborhood, the park was a good place to bring their dogs to play, and quite a few adults would gather to watch the baseball games.

But the park was suddenly closed just before the beginning of summer vacation, when schoolchildren would be out playing in this park in earnest. Legions of bulldozers and dumptrucks came in their place, constructing a city park. Construction went on for a year and a half after that. The grass fields were dug up, the sides of the fields were surrounded with concrete walls and the bleachers replaced, so that the place looked like a magnificent racetrack replete with grandstands. The small spaces off to the sides were replaced with brick-enclosed flower beds ("no admittance"), tennis courts, croquet grounds, and exercise grounds.

The city had spent some four billion yen on the park up to that point. It was planning to spend an additional six billion to turn the site into a major city park.

I went with Takashi one day to see a part of the new park that had been opened. At the entrance was a huge sign, almost as if the city fathers had erected it as a warning to the residents. No CATS OR DOGS ALLOWED, it read, in big red and black letters.

"What does it say?" Takashi asked me.

"It says that dogs and cats are not allowed in this park."

"Oh," he said. He seemed to be thinking about something.

"But that's strange," he said, after a while.

"Why?"

"Because dogs and cats can't read!"

But of course! I thought. Most of the time dogs are taken for walks on a leash, so the owners, at least, will see this sign. Cats, however, usually come and go as they please. "You're right," I said with a laugh. "Cats can't read."

"What a stupid sign," said Takashi. He had recently learned how to write and not just print, and he laughed pleasantly, pleased with himself for being at least a little smarter than a cat.

Still, the city's usual display of abrupt discourtesy and a penchant for prohibiting admittance to anything and everything—as evidenced by this No Pets sign—struck me as ridiculous; at the same time, it made me boil with anger.

The bleachers had been turned into something like an all-purpose playing field. On the other side of the grass was a 300-meter track, at one end of which was something extraordinary—a shot-put circle like the ones usually found on practice fields at schools built long ago.

"Hey, Takashi, this is where they have the shot-put competitions."

He didn't seem very interested in it. On the other side of the park, a helicopter hovered over the forest of ginkgo trees where a gymnasium was going to be built. As I was walking past the shot-put circle, it dawned on me that, although this was supposed to be a city park, a park for all the people of the city, its planners appeared to have done their level best to ignore the wishes and needs of those people—of us. I felt disgusted. After all, how many shot-putters could there be in this city, anyway? Instead of taking all that space to accommodate at most one or maybe two competitions a year between a very limited number of people, wouldn't it have been better to make some space for children and pets to play and run around in at will? As I thought about these things while we walked, the thought of living in this town began to depress me.

Spring vacation ended, and Takashi started the second grade. I realized then that, in the end, I had never actually asked Takashi himself why he hit his classmates all during the time he was in first grade. I excused myself by saying that he'd done well enough in a year, considering that he was the only one in a class of thirty-four children who had been illiterate to begin with, that boys have their own problems to deal with when growing up, and so on.

Even in the second grade, for Takashi the best thing about going to school continued to be the chance to play with his friends. Every day, he and his friends seemed to find some new place to play and to do something different. At night, when I gave him his bath, he'd talk about what he'd done that day. It was at about this time that the name Takayama, a classmate of Takashi's of whom I'd not heard previously, began to crop up frequently. From what

Takashi told me, I learned that Takayama had transferred into the second grade from another school; he and Takashi were in the same class. Takashi had mentioned Takayama when he told me about having hit Yuji.

"Takayama-kun knows a lot about fishing," Takashi said, as happy as if he had been talking about himself and with a funny kind of pride. "He has a brother in the fifth grade, and he says that his father takes them fishing a lot. There are a lot of really big fishing poles at his home." That's when he started going over to Takayama's house to play.

Takayama seemed to be a very generous boy. Every time Takashi came home from the Takayamas', he'd have some barbless fishhooks, or fishing line, or some outrageously big floats, or plastic models.

"You're always receiving a lot of different things from Takayama, but are you giving him anything in return?" I asked Takashi one day as we were walking through the woods near Central Park.

"Yeah, I gave him a metal erector set once," Takashi said. "But Takayama-kun seems to like giving me things more."

The park itself was closed off with ugly steel fencing of the kind used for construction sites, and the woods had been reduced to about half its former size. But the citron tree that Takashi and I were looking for that day was still there, covered with a thin layer of dust but otherwise standing aloof somewhat comically, as if at a loss for something to do.

"It's here! It's still here!" Takashi shouted as he swiftly circled its trunk. Bunches of caterpillars crawled about all but unseen on the undersides of the dark green leaves and between the stems, clustering there like lumps of salt and pepper scattered about.

We put about two dozen caterpillars in a paper bag, together with a bunch of citron leaves for food. Raising larvae and watching them change into butterflies was a big thing with kids just then.

"Is Takayama raising any butterflies?" I asked.

"No. He and his brother keep tropical fish. He's got a big aquarium full of them. He says his father buys them in foreign countries."

As we walked, I placed the bag close to Takashi's ear.

"I can hear them!" he cried. "I can hear them eating the leaves!"

I met Takayama for the first time the following Saturday. He had a sort of toy pistol in his right hand and a fishing rod—with reel and lure—in his left. He was only about half as big as Takashi and wore shorts with an apple design on them, which I thought was a little too young for a boy in the second grade. In complete contrast to Takashi, he wore his hair straight down in a bowl cut, which made him look like a little girl. The two of them standing together made an odd sight.

"You must be Takayama-kun," I said, sticking my head out from the living room. "Come inside."

"Excuse me," he said politely, in a high, slightly reedy voice. He took off his shoes.

"Did you make that pistol yourself?" I asked.

"Yes, I did," he answered.

I wanted to ask him to show me the gun so I could see how it was made, but he acted so adult for a second-grader that I decided against it. I found it hard to talk with him freely. If he had said "Yeah" or "Yeah, ya wanna see it?" things would have gone differently.

"Takashi's always getting some present from you, so I'll make you some *yakisoba* to eat later, OK?" I said. The boy had such an adult manner of answering me that I couldn't help talking to him in the same way.

"Thank you," he said, in his high-pitched voice. He followed Takashi upstairs. I couldn't help wondering if all second-graders said "Excuse me" when they went inside somebody else's home. Then I thought about my own son, my irreverent little Takashi, and I became very worried. I made a mental note to ask him about this after Takayama left, but that day I was distracted by other things and forgot about it.

"The incident" occurred about a month after the start of school, with a phone call from the school.

"I'm sorry to inconvenience you, but could you come over right away?" It was Yamagishi, the teacher. His voice was low and muffled, as if he had been talking through his hand into the receiver.

I relayed the message to my wife, who had gone to work early that day and had only just come home, also early. She became tense. "I wonder what it could be?"

"If it were an injury, the teacher would have spoken with more urgency, so I don't think it's something like that," I said.

About an hour later my wife came back with Takashi. She looked thoroughly exhausted, and the base of her nose was red. She waited for Takashi to go to his room upstairs.

"They said Takashi stole his friend's money." She spoke rapidly, in a whisper.

"What?" I said, incredulous. Though I'd been worried, I'd expected something no worse than Takashi's fighting with someone or having a trick he'd played exposed.

"Takayama's mother came in with this desperate look," my wife went on. "She said that, lately, the boy's brother's allowance had been disappearing quite often, and when she questioned Takayama about it yesterday, he said that Takashi had been stealing it."

"They said Takashi's been going into Takayama's house and stealing it?" I asked, still amazed. As I listened, for some reason I felt like laughing.

"That's what they said. His mother said her kids had no reason to steal, and she gave me a really threatening look!"

"I can't believe this."

"Neither can I, just suddenly being accused like that. I also thought we'd really have to ask Takashi himself."

"What did the teacher say?" I asked.

"He said we should all investigate the matter."

I even felt exasperated at how quickly I began to feel deeply unhappy inside.

"I wonder how Mrs. Takayama can be so sure Takashi stole the money," I said, realizing that it was this point that made me feel so uncomfortable.

"She says that that's what Takayama-kun told her when she questioned him about it."

Takayama's bowl-cut head appeared briefly in my mind and then disappeared. The sum stolen was ¥500, a fresh new note that the boy's brother had been planning to put in the bank. Money wasn't the only thing to have disappeared, according to Mrs. Takayama. Artificial bait and floats that the elder Takayama prized had been missing frequently, and it looked as if Takashi had stolen these items, too. She wouldn't have felt so bad, she said, in a shrill voice heightened with agitation, if only these things had been involved. But stealing money at such an early age was a serious matter.

As I listened to my wife tell me all this, I felt a pain in the left side of my chest. I'd always heard that extraordinary apprehension or anger can cause chest pains, and the thought that this was apparently true remained vaguely in my mind like a monotonous soliloquy.

That night, in the bath, I suddenly asked: "Listen, Takashi, have you ever taken anything like fishhooks or money from the Takayamas' without asking anybody's permission?"

I tried to ask this question in as normal an intonation as possible, in a slightly clumsy, intentionally joking manner.

"Yep," he said with alacrity, making a big bubble out of his washcloth.

I felt my stomach sink.

"Without asking permission?" I said quickly.

"But I wasn't the one who took it. Takayama-kun just brings the stuff to me. He says it's all right. Then he gives it all to me."

"Money too?"

"Yep. Last time he brought five hundred and thirty yen."

"What did you do with it?"

"Four of us—Kei-chan, Imai's older brother, me and Takayama—hit the *gacha-gacha* at Medakaya."

"You spent the whole five hundred and thirty on that?"

"Yep. We had about three turns apiece. Imai's brother got mad when he got the same thing three times in a row, and he shook the machine, and a guy from the store came over and hollered at him. I'm pretty good at it, so I got what I wanted all three times."

Takashi was completely casual about it. This *gacha-gacha* is a kind of vending machine filled with toys in plastic containers that you can get by depositing twenty or thirty yen. The catch is that you don't always get the toy you want.

"That money and fishing tackle don't belong to Takayama, Takashi. They belong to his brother. So from now on don't take them, even if he gives them to you." This time I spoke a little severely.

"Why?" he asked.

"Because it's wrong. Especially money—you shouldn't take money from friends."

"OK. I won't," he said right away.

"Have you ever had a fight with Takayama?"

"No, never."

"Did you ever hit him?"

"Nope. Why should I? He's my friend."

"I guess so. Are you the strongest in your class, Takashi?"

"Yep."

"Strongest in your grade?"

"Yeah, either me or Kyoichi in the second class. Kyoichi's pretty strong, too." He answered in an almost matter-of-fact tone. I hadn't taught him anything in the way of studies, I thought. Instead, I'd wrestled with him and boxed and played at karate with him, and nothing else. Now, he's training himself in these areas all by himself. This realization gave me a strange feeling.

My wife told me to meet with Takashi's teacher, so three days later I went to see him at his home. I thought I'd get the details of the various troubles my son's behavior was probably causing on a daily basis, and make some sort of general apology.

"Well, he's still just a child. Almost everybody does something like this once or twice in his life, as a kind of test," Yamagishi said, with all the calm confidence of a veteran teacher of fifty years or more.

I didn't clearly understand what exactly was supposed to be a test of what. As we talked, however, I realized that this Yamagishi had concluded that, as far as "the incident" was concerned, Takashi was thoroughly guilty of theft. What is going on here? I wondered, frankly amazed, as I listened to Yamagishi speak like a Sunday pastor delivering a sermon to a wayward disciple. I thought that this guy was really something else.

I felt as if my talk with Takashi in the bath three days earlier had confirmed my suspicions. As Takashi's father I couldn't say so, but I had thought all along that Takayama, that delicate-looking transfer-student with the bowl cut, had been currying favor with his new classmates by getting the strongest kid in the class into trouble.

The more I thought about what Takayama's mother had said—that my lackadaisical son had sneaked into her elder son's room like a professional thief and stolen a brand-new ¥500 note out of a desk drawer—the more absurd, even unreal, I found the scenario she'd described. Why would a boy who doesn't even use his monthly allowance of ¥150 but just leaves the coins scattered around on his desk go into someone else's home to steal money? The thought made me quake with anger inside.

"Well, as long as all the parents involved see to it that this sort of thing doesn't happen again, I see no need to pursue the matter any further," Yamagishi said, with an air of importance. His eyes gleamed behind his glasses. He finally lit the cigarette he'd been toying with for so long.

Later that night, I didn't even wait for my wife to change clothes after coming home from work before telling her about my conversation with Yamagishi.

"It's terrible, making Takashi out to be a thief like that," I said to her. I felt indescribably empty inside.

As always, Takashi and I went into the bath before dinner, talking about nothing in particular.

"When I checked the box today, I found eighteen pupae," he said, pouring hot water over his shoulders and slowly shaking his head from side to side. "Three more are still larvae, so I guess they died."

"Oh? That was quick!"

"Yeah. That's because I gave them a lot of food every day. The ones that ate a lot turned into pupae first. Komatsu-kun and Maa-chan say theirs have turned into pupae, too, but I think mine'll turn into butterflies before anyone else's."

"I see."

"Then Takayama-kun wanted to give me some hairstreak pupae, but I told them I didn't want them. They're not worth it." At this he wrinkled his nose in a gesture so adult I just had to laugh.

"So they're not worth it?" I asked.

"Yeah, they're so small."

Exactly one week later all the pupae in Takashi's box metamorphosed into swallowtails.

"I did it, Dad!" Takashi came tumbling down the stairs waving his right hand in a circle. He seemed truly happy.

"Right now there are thirteen of them," he said. "At this rate they might all turn into butterflies."

I went upstairs to my son's room to find a commotion of black and yellow blurs that filled the interior of a small box on the desk. That tiny little box trembled and shook from side to side, and looked as if it might itself take flight at any moment.

"It's amazing how fast they turned into swallowtails," Takashi said, taking the box in his hands. He stood there, clearly but happily perplexed about what to do next.

All eighteen swallowtail pupae changed into butterflies overnight. The little box soon proved too small for them; they barely had room to spread their wings and move around. The next day at about noon, Takashi stood on the veranda of his room on the second floor and released them. At first, the newly metamorphosed swallowtails simply continued to flit about in vain inside the box, unable to find the entrance. Suddenly, two or three of the butterflies perched on the edge of the tiny square opening, stayed there a moment, then finally flew off into the hot, humid sunlight of an early summer day.

"Fly! Fly away!" Takashi shouted, pulling the swallowtails out into the air as he held the box on the far side of the railing.

Several more swallowtails appeared on the other side of the boy with the shaved head, beating their wings ceaselessly as they flew off into the midday summer sun.

Translated by Joseph Farrar

GOD IS NOWHERE; GOD IS NOW HERE

Itoh Seikoh

NOTED SINCE HIS STUDENT DAYS FOR HIS NEW AND UNIQUE FORMAT AS A STAND-UP COMEDIAN, ITOH SEIKOH HAS BEEN ACTIVE IN A WIDE VARIETY OF MEDIA. HE HAS BEEN THE HOST OF A NATIONALLY BROADCAST PROGRAM AND HAS BEEN CALLED ONE OF JAPAN'S REPRESENTATIVE RAP ARTISTS FOR HIS RUN-DMC AND PUBLIC ENEMY ACTS. HE HAS APPEARED ON STAGE AND IN VIDEO AS A MEMBER OF THE RADICAL GAZIBERIBIMBA SYSTEM, A COMEDY TEAM. HIS **NO LIFE KING,** A CYBER-REALISTIC PORTRAYAL OF NINTENDO KIDS, BECAME A NATIONAL BEST SELLER.

It was at Xmas.

A relative had died, and I had gone home to my parents' house.

There I was, back in my old room again. I went rooting through my things, pulling out this and that. It worked out that I spent a long time doing it.

God Is Nowhere; God Is Now Here

My brain was numb from the cheap grain alcohol that had been served, round after round, at the funeral, but something my uncle said had stuck in my mind. My uncle lived in the next town, and he had been his usual mean and obnoxious self. There was something about the *way* he had spoken to me. It wouldn't let go of me, and that was probably why I had thrown myself into this business with such vengeance.

I had worked through the night, being careful not to disturb my parents, who were snoring away downstairs. It was five in the morning before I reached the inner recesses of the closet, and crawling on my knees, I unearthed such artifacts as a bent spoon and a miniature flashlight bulb that we had used in shop class.

And out of the deepest alluvium of old memories I excavated a magnifying glass.

No need to subject it to X rays for dating: I could identify without question the day and age when it had lived on this earth. Namely, Showa 45. That was 1970. I was in the fourth grade.

The lens came into my possession one day shortly before Xmas that year.

My memory is quite clear about it: there were four of us in our gang—Shin, Maru, Mitsugu, and myself. The city was alive with a holiday mood. But we were angry with the world and feeling peculiarly hyper.

We had just gotten caught and reported for setting off a rocket firecracker. We had fired it through the open window of an apartment building.

As if it were not enough to have the homeroom teacher show up, even the principal came. They dragged us off to the apartment and made us apologize to the young couple who lived there.

I remember the walk home afterward. The evening sky bore down on us and seemed ready to crush us with its weight. But we were angry and determined not to give in. Shin, who was the ringleader of our gang, tried to cheer us up.

"We can be proud of ourselves. We were tough and took our punishment, didn't we? But that couple—they're wimps who wouldn't think twice about having a fight in broad daylight right in front of everybody. You think they have any pride?"

"You said it, Shin. They deserved what we did to them," Maru chimed in. His shoulders were thrown back in anger, but there was something too heavy, and uncommonly forced, about the sound of his voice. Especially for a fourth-grader.

He was not alone in this. All of us were trying too hard to pretend we were adults.

We recognized only the strong, and held the weak in unmitigated contempt. That was the morality we had adopted for ourselves. And we had come to believe that we, and we alone, were capable of maintaining this code.

Naturally, we reserved our greatest scorn for the likes of a woman who shrieked her head off over a little firecracker thrown in her apartment window. And for the teacher, or the principal, whose sole reaction to the incident was to apologize, oblivious to whether it was the woman, or her slightly soiled apron, to which they bowed repeatedly.

Nonetheless, we were filled with pain, and pain to the bursting point. We kept walking with no direction in mind. No one tried to go home.

I was the first to notice the little boy.

A very small boy.

He was riding a pink pig hunkered down at the entrance to the park. One of the boy's hands was extended in our direction. He sat perfectly still. He appeared to be made of the same concrete as the pig.

"Look at that, will you? Real weird."

I had opened my mouth without thinking of the consequences.

The boy looked like a baby doll. He had a very white complexion, and his forehead protruded oddly from a mass of soft curls that covered his head. Moreover, he held a plastic magnifying glass in his right hand that he extended toward us. He was looking at us through the lens.

"Hey, Mitsugu. Let's give him a scare."

Shin was talking. Mitsugu was the smallest of the four of us. He was the one who always had to play messenger boy for Shin.

"What's with you, kid?"

But the little boy did not reply in spite of Mitsugu's attempts to provoke him. Nor was there any change in the vague smile on the boy's face.

He simply continued to hold up the magnifying glass, and struggling ineptly to keep one eye shut, tried to focus on Mitsugu.

Maru laughed at Mitsugu when Mitsugu flinched and turned away.

"You looked like a POW with a gun pointed at your head."

But Maru fell into a silent funk when he realized the lens had been turned on him too.

"Think he's a first-grader?"

Shin was talking to me. Now the little boy was focusing the lens on Shin.

"I didn't ask *you*, idiot."

Shin was shouting. Things were getting serious. I wanted to warn the little boy how cruel Shin could be when he got mad.

"Never seen him before. He's too big to be in the Midori Day School. Probably not a transfer from another school, either."

I tried to speak as matter-of-factly as possible. Just so Shin wouldn't get any crazy ideas.

It was already too late.

Shin clawed at the back of his darkly complected neck. He was concocting some sort of plan. The makings of a lynching, no doubt.

The little boy perceived nothing. He continued to smile.

I was afraid. But in Shin's presence, there was no way I might admit to anything even vaguely suggestive of fear. Do that, and Shin would lynch *me*. I kept my eyes directed to the ground and said nothing. Maru and Mitsugu did the same.

The area behind the metal works was already dark. There was only the light from the houses on the other side of the wall to see by as Shin went about his business. He had pulled a plastic bag out of a trash can in the park, and into it he patiently emptied a container of toluene. We stood there watching passively, even as we choked on the fumes.

The lynching began.

Mitsugu's hands were shaking. The little boy had been stretched out face up on a sheet of cardboard. It was Mitsugu's job to lower the plastic bag and hold it directly over the boy's face.

The little boy did not resist. To the contrary, he made a point of bravely extending his right arm and holding the magnifying glass higher. He studied our faces one by one. He even smiled at us.

"Take a look at this jerk, will you. He can't even figure out what is about to happen to him."

Shin was talking as he got to his feet.

"If you don't like it, say so! That's the way it is with you wimps. And look at that asinine grin on his face. That's why it's so easy for us to do him in. We're the strong ones."

But Shin's knees were shaking, and I was struggling desperately to fight back the fear I felt as I stood there holding down the little boy's left arm. I suspect Maru, who had been told to hold the boy's legs, was on the verge of crying, too. Although the boy offered no resistance, Maru had spread-eagled himself over the boy's legs so that I couldn't see his face.

"Dumb wimp. Say something."

Shin had pushed Mitsugu aside, along with the bag of toluene he held in his hand, and jumped on top of the boy.

"You're going to die, idiot. Get the picture? You want us to save you, right? Then, say something!"

The little boy's large eyes were like empty cavities. Nonetheless, he raised his right hand so that he could study Shin's face with the magnifying glass.

"You don't want to die, huh?"

We stood there staring at the boy, hoping that his thin lips would move and he would say something. But he did no more than let the corners of his mouth curl into a faint smile.

"So you *do* want to die, after all?"

How can I forget the look on the little boy's face just then? It defied description. Neither was it a reply to Shin's question, nor was it a matter of wanting, or not wanting, to die. He just smiled. It was as simple as that. Moreover, the smile meant nothing— neither a belief that his life would be spared nor a seeking of release by abandoning all hope. He merely turned and gave us a smile.

I lifted the magnifying glass in the cold air and let the lens come back to life after a lapse of seventeen years. I looked out the window.

The lens did not reflect the landscape, reversing it as in a looking glass.

It had remained unchanged: it was the same as it was when the little boy possessed it.

It was still a reject—a dud—that will never know the perfection of being in focus. The only worlds to be grasped in its silent reflection will remain forever vague and indistinct.

Translated by William J. Tyler

X-RATED BLANKET

Eimi Yamada

EIMI YAMADA WAS BORN IN 1959 IN TOKYO AND MAJORED IN
LITERATURE AT MEIJI UNIVERSITY. HER **BEDDO TAIMU AIZU
(BED TIME EYES)** WON THE BUNGEI AWARD. SHE WAS NOM-
INATED FOR THE AKUTAGAWA AWARD IN 1985 FOR THAT
WORK, AND AGAIN IN SUCCESSIVE YEARS FOR HER NOVELS
JESSI NO SEBONE (JESSY'S BACKBONE) AND **CHO-CHO NO
TENSOKU (BUTTERFLY'S FOOT-BINDING)**. HER **SOUL MUSIC-
LOVERS ONLY** RECEIVED THE NINETY-SEVENTH NAOKI
AWARD.

When I say I want a man, I mean this man; if it's not that man,
then it just won't do for me. George. The name alone twists open
a faucet inside my body. Twisted, I am wet; water floods high
enough to wet my eyes. That's how I clearly recognize my own
desire when I look in the mirror.

Powdering myself, applying lipstick, I suddenly halt my hand,
remembering many things. These memories frighten me a little
because they so resemble flashbacks—the final-stage symptoms
suffered by drug addicts. The name George is the key which
opens my body. I whisper that name, and my legs open of themselves; I place my hand there, inside, churning what is about to
ooze out. I blend this self, a self excited by a finger. And so in a
delicious state a delicious concoction is served up; how wasteful
that George is not here. I close my eyes in distress.

Ever since I met George I am always starved and wretched. No matter how often I hold him, or how much I am held, the next moment brings fresh desire for George. He never extinguishes the spark of desire inside me. He was the first man to impart memory to my body itself. My skin retains the sensation of becoming saturated by his; I can always remember this clearly. This astonishes me. That the physical can imprint so strongly on the physical. I didn't realize until then that a specific man's body could become an essential for a woman.

I think that George experiences me in the same way. The doorbell rings; I fly to the door. The knob rattles noisily with my impatience as I open the door. Together with the outside air George's eyes nestle into my body. I receive, catch his tumbling gaze. Before being touched by fingers or lips, all of me is licked by his eyes.

George does not push me down. In spite of that my body collapses weakly into a shape mirroring the space between his arms. Like mine, his body caves and coils. When my skin makes a depression, his skin touching that spot rises to fill it in. When my nipples are erect they are buried by his body. We love each other exactly like liquids. Feeling that we both are entwined together in everything, I am overtaken with a desire to weep. That we are each others' perfecting part. I cannot separate this man from myself.

All we ever do is make love. Maybe I will suffer divine punishment for calling it love. But we cannot do anything about it. We cannot endure not dissolving into one another when we are separated, and of course when together we simply must shed our clothes rapidly. We become crazed with impatience. From the first time we shared a bed our bodies have been tugging against each others'—webs sweet as honey. We live dragging this dripping pleasure, a pleasure that can never be sated.

I dress myself so George may desire me at any moment. I even wash carefully between my toes so that he may, at any time, take them in his mouth. Of course I polish my toenails. I wonder if I am the only woman to go as far as perfuming her toes. I labor to make myself into a delicious treat for him. He might want to bite my neck sometime, so I take special care of it. Baked to a soft brown in the sun, prepared in advance ready to be eaten any time. I always adorn my earlobes with gold pierced earrings so that his tongue may savor them. When putting on my makeup I agonize over such details as which lipstick, which blush will make me the most beautiful as I lie in George's arms. This is how I serve him.

Sometimes we talk frankly.

"All we do is make love."

"We can't help it. We have to make love."

"Why do we have to make love?"

"Because I love you."

George's eyes are already moist as he answers. His lips close firmly to prevent his desire from spilling out. I think: he wants me. Even as I am wondering if he does, already my body is encompassed by his skin. Warm, heavy. I feel peaceful. Reassurance awakens my sensuality, and I am hot down to my tiptoes.

I think that using the phrase "in love" is appropriate. I believe that it is OK to use such lofty words for something that is an absolute necessity. If I were not enwrapped by George's body, my life would probably be ruined by my fretfulness. Even if I am left breathless by the onslaught of pleasure, without him I could have no tranquillity.

Maybe people will say we are like animals. But do animals desire their partners like this? Can they know the art of feeling the flesh tingle with desire even as one is satisfied? Every bit of him is enveloped in smooth skin. There, in that core, he is. Can an animal hunger to taste that, as though sipping broth? I want George. I want only him.

Wrapped in his two arms I am helpless. Although he is never violent, I find it hard to breathe. I search around in desperation, as if I were drowning. If there is a pillow, I seize the pillow; if the sheets have wrinkled, I cling to them. Sometimes, during such moments I catch sight of his hands. Bony, thick fingers. The thought of the largeness of his fingernails makes me shiver uncontrollably. I realize that this body draped over mine is a completely different type of body. I move my hips, raise my voice, trying to transform his type into the same type as mine.

George likes whispers. His voice is always cool. That troubles me. I express my pleasure openly; he is not like that. It excites me more and more. A man who is without a modicum of rationality in bed will disillusion a woman. At such times a woman likes to be treated with a touch of unkindness. Even though she is completely absorbed, she enjoys a bit of teasing, a little naughtiness.

In those moments his whispering voice contains fingers and arms, even a tongue. It has a genius for everything: pinching my ears, opening my pores, tickling my sides. This, crowned with sweet words or vulgar queries, seizes my heart and reduces me to tears. At these times the word "love" by itself turns into a tool which moves the lower half of my body. It is his words, even more than his penis, that turn into a naughty toy which makes me wild, makes me salivate. This is loving. My artless mind thinks so: the grinding of naked bodies against each other, leaking, sparking, blending, all of this. Is there any finer way to love? Crying, yelling, laughing. These things all happen at once; is there anything else so preposterous? George's whispers make me crazy. The tone of his delicate voice, incongruous with his large body, makes me do all things. As soon as his low, soft voice passes into and through my ears, it is transformed to a yell of desperation. The cool whisper of a man dampens a woman's ears, still and quiet, where it becomes a broadcast. He can do that. Only through me as filter.

I think I need redden only my lips. He will do the rest for me.

He stains me red here and there. My skin turns red in those spots where he bites and sucks. He pulls up hot blood from inside me and leaves it floating, revealed, on the surface of my skin. I wonder if he wants to eat me up, speeding the pounding in my breast. Little by little my whole body is colored. I will take care of the lips on my face by myself, but the rest of me I will leave to him, and then, at that moment when words fail me, he is probably dying red those lips which hold his penis. By the time droplets drip down on me from his sweat-soaked brow, my entire body has already been colored. Perfect physicality is, in this way, fully consummated. As the sensation of satiation fills me—the satisfaction of having at last become one—I savor an intense pleasure tinged already with the mingling of a new, ongoing hunger.

George's voice flows on composedly as always, like the strains of a southern melody, but I am sure that he feels just as good as I do. I know this because his skin is puckered with gooseflesh even though his body is scorched with heat. This is evidence of a physical response, specific to human beings who have been touched by keen emotion. I then stroke George's body as though I were comforting a child who has put on a display of bravery. Just like a child who, desperately enduring loneliness, will burst into tears at a single gentle word, he, unable to resist, breathes a single deep sigh. Precious George. Precious me. I stroke his back for a while, savoring our shared satisfaction. In his satisfaction he allows the strength to go out of his body, temporarily defenseless. It is only then that I feel again and accept the heaviness of his body. Beloved. I love him. Too precious to strip off, he is like my blanket.

Translated by Nina Cornyetz

YU-HEE

Yang Ji Lee

YANG JI LEE WAS BORN IN 1955 IN YAMANASHI-KEN. SHE
WROTE HER FIRST NOVEL, **NABI TARYUNG (A LAMENTING
BUTTERFLY**), WHILE SHE WAS A STUDENT AT THE LANGUAGE-
PREPARATION SCHOOL OF SEOUL UNIVERSITY; THE WORK
WAS LATER PUBLISHED BY **GUNZO,** A MONTHLY LITERARY
MAGAZINE FROM TOKYO. IN 1984 SHE RETURNED TO SEOUL
UNIVERSITY FROM JAPAN AND GRADUATED IN 1988. SHE
CURRENTLY IS IN GRADUATE SCHOOL AT EWHA WOMEN'S
COLLEGE, SEOUL, WHERE HER FIELD OF RESEARCH IS THE
RELATIONSHIP BETWEEN BUDDHISM AND DANCE. HER MOST
RECENT NOVEL, **YU-HEE,** WAS PUBLISHED BY **GUNZO** IN
1988 AND RECEIVED THE 1989 AKUTAGAWA AWARD. THIS
STORY IS AN EXCERPT FROM THAT NOVEL.

The wind was still strong. The windows shook, and the sound of
the swirling wind beating on the glass echoed throughout the
living room.

My aunt stretched her legs out on the floor and began to massage her left knee. She had been silent for a while, but now she
began to speak.

"You know, as soon as Yu-Hee arrived in this country, the picture of Korea that she had painted in her mind was shattered. I
think that's why she even came to hate the Korean language. Languages are like that.

"Your uncle told me something before he died. Throughout
his *tongne,* the village where he was born, in Kyŏngsang Prov-

ince, there was strong anti-Japanese sentiment, ever since the time of Japanese imperialism. Many of the famous fighters in the anti-Japanese resistance came from that *tongne*. So, your uncle said, it was probably because he was born there, and his *abŏji* (father, in Korean) had such strong anti-Japanese feelings, and he was brought up in that environment, that he just couldn't get rid of his prejudice. For over ten years, he went to Japan once or twice a year on business, but he never learned to speak Japanese fluently. Though he could read and write, he was just hopeless when it came to speaking. Perhaps this was because of the feelings that had grown deep in his subconscious. Anyway, he didn't have any special desire to speak Japanese well. But he would often say how annoyed he was with himself about that.

"My daughter and I were influenced by him, without even being aware of it. We just couldn't bring ourselves to like Japanese people. My daughter absolutely refused to take Japanese as her second language. And I'll bet that's why. Somehow, I think I understand Yu-Hee. I feel very sad about her. I simply can't think of her as a stranger. I can't remember when it was that I really got to thinking about this. My husband and Yu-Hee were of different generations, but they attended the same university. I don't know what fate brought Yu-Hee to live here in this house, but I thought how strange it was—these two compatriots—one hating Japan, and the other hating Korea."

I understood very well what my aunt was talking about. To me, too, the "fate" seemed apt. Only, my feelings were not clear-cut. I searched for words and tried to find some way to express my own burdensome thoughts. Yu-Hee noticed only the negative aspects of Korea. Since she had grown up hearing her father criticize Korea, she hated even the Korean language. But I couldn't help thinking, it can't be that simple. I couldn't believe that Yu-Hee's obsession with the Japanese language resulted from her aversion to Korean.

Then I recalled the sheaf of papers that Yu-Hee had left behind, now put away in a drawer of the desk. The pages filled with her Japanese characters appeared vividly in my memory. I pictured Yu-Hee squeezed into that tiny space, bent over her desk, writing her Japanese while listening to her *taegum* records and gazing at the instrument on her right.

That uncomfortable, unsettling sensation, like heartburn, was still there.

My aunt continued to massage her knee, facing the television set. Her knee had started hurting her about a month ago. She no longer climbed the mountain behind the house. She made no attempt to turn up the volume. I knew she wasn't watching. I wondered what memory of Yu-Hee was going through her mind. Which of Yu-Hee's words or gestures was she remembering?

"You know, Yu-Hee always refused to watch television."

As she spoke, my aunt slowly raised her left knee. Then she stretched her leg out again, slowly, and started rubbing her knee.

"Your uncle told me how impressed he was the first time he saw color television, on one of his first business trips to Japan. But he had no desire to watch it. He said that he couldn't bear the sound of the Japanese language coming out of the television set. You know, Yu-Hee never made any attempt to watch television, either. I was always telling her that she should. I told her that watching television is a good way to learn the language, and that historical dramas teach you a lot about history. Whenever there was a good program on, I would tell her about it. But she never came downstairs to watch—not even once. When I remembered what your uncle had told me, I gradually came to understand why."

There was a brief silence.

"I never told Yu-Hee this, but I was secretly cheering her on. In my mind, I was constantly saying to her, 'It won't be much longer. Once you overcome these painful feelings, everything will be just fine. Japan is no different from Korea. What is really important is to pay close attention to how other people are living, and to think carefully about what you want to do with your own life. You just need a little more patience until you get to that point.' I was always on her side."

After she finished speaking, my aunt still seemed to be contemplating her words. Then she nodded any number of times, as if in approval of what she had just said.

I remained silent. Though the Yu-Hee whom my aunt had known and the Yu-Hee whom I had known may have been two different people, I agreed with my aunt. This was Yu-Hee's own problem. No matter how much we worried about her, or encouraged her, Yu-Hee had to think and feel for herself and develop her own strength. I couldn't believe that she was a weak person. Suddenly the thought came to me that perhaps her suffering stemmed from her youth, and I was going to mention this to my aunt, but swallowed my words.

Yu-Hee's room was diagonally above the living room. Whenever there was an interesting program on television, my aunt would tell her. But, while the two of us watched it, in the same house, at the same time, Yu-Hee was probably doing her Japanese writing. That mental picture prevented me from speaking and made me feel uneasy and suffocated.

The noise made by the wind drowned out the sound of the television set with the volume turned down. The windows rattled, and soon a misty rain started to fall.

I said "Why don't I cut us an apple?" and went into the kitchen. When I returned to the living room, I sat down facing my aunt and put the tray with the apple on it on the floor.

As I pared the apple, I said, "I wonder if Yu-Hee has arrived at her home in Tokyo."

"Well, she said it takes three hours from Narita. So, if the plane took off right on schedule at four o'clock, it should arrive at Narita airport at six o'clock. Yes, I'll bet she's arriving at Narita right about now."

"Do you suppose it's raining in Japan, too?"

My aunt looked up at the window, and as she answered "Yes, that's possible," her voice sounded hollow, as though she were lost in thought.

"What do you think Yu-Hee will do, first thing, when she arrives in Japan?"

"Well . . ."

I stifled a laugh. I had the vague feeling that the lump in my chest was moving. I felt sad, choked sobs bouncing off the tiny lump and sinking into my chest. And then, for some unknown reason, Yu-Hee's sobs and the pain in my chest turned into laughter, which I suppressed.

"Aunt, I think that the first thing that girl is going to do when she gets home is watch television!"

Then I burst out laughing. My aunt, falling in with my mood, said, "That's right. I'll bet you're right," and then she, too, burst out laughing, though with a puzzled, pained expression on her face.

"Aunt, do you remember the time Yu-Hee pared an apple? It looked like this. See?"

I purposely pared the apple so that a lot of meat came off with the skin, and made cuts which ran every which way. I picked up a piece of skin about five centimeters long, and held it up for my aunt to see. She laughed, this time with a cheerful expression on her face. We laughed together, each of us recalling Yu-Hee doing the very same thing in the past.

It was right here in this living room that, one day when I was paring an apple, the idea occurred to me to ask Yu-Hee to do it. Whenever Yu-Hee wanted an apple, she would always bring it to me or my aunt, and say, "Would you pare this for me?" I didn't think she asked us because she couldn't do it herself. My aunt felt the same way—this was just one facet of Yu-Hee, the childish one.

Yu-Hee tried to get out of doing it, saying that she would waste too much of the apple. But I finally persuaded her to do it.

Soon, a jagged, five-centimeter-long paring fell down with a thump. I held the knife precariously.

"*Kulonika, akapchanayo!* See, I told you I would waste it!"

I continued to imitate Yu-Hee, pursing my lips, pronouncing my words awkwardly, and hunching my shoulders. My aunt continued to laugh for some time.

The raindrops were larger now. I thought, "It will probably rain all night. Maybe the weather will be nice tomorrow. I wonder if it's raining in Japan?"

When my aunt had stopped laughing, she caught her breath and picked up a piece of apple stuck on a toothpick. Then she sighed deeply, and ate the piece of apple. We shared the apple, as we listened to the rain in silence. On the tray, along with the other parings, was the small piece of skin that evoked Yu-Hee.

"What's going to happen to that girl now? She dropped out of her Japanese college, and now she's dropped out of Seoul University. . . . I hope she meets a nice man. If she doesn't, then marriage will pass her by, just like what happened to you."

My aunt glared at me when I laughed. I took the paring that I had cut earlier, when I was imitating Yu-Hee, from the tray, and held it up.

I said, "She'll have to find a man who doesn't eat apples," and my aunt forced a laugh.

I don't know why, but at that moment, I remembered the sight of the mountain beyond the hilly road. I choked up. The tiny lump seemed to have expanded suddenly.

"Aunt, Yu-Hee will be all right. Someday she'll come to visit us with her husband and children. You'll see."

The vision of the mountain persisted, flickering before my eyes.

My aunt said, "I wonder if Yu-Hee will come to Korea again. I wonder if she'll come to see us."

I answered, "She will. I'm sure she will." Whatever it was—this powerful force building up inside me—seemed to be compelling my body to move. I edged over next to my aunt, and started to massage her knee for her.

The volume on the television set had been turned down, leaving only the picture. Outside, the rain was pouring down. Huge raindrops hit the window and bounced off. It sounded like water being thrown at the window.

My aunt left the curtain at the entrance to the living room open, and brought the telephone in from its usual place right next to the front door. She set the telephone on the floor and sat down in front of it.

"When my daughter answers, I'll talk to her first, and afterward, you can talk to her, all right?"

As she spoke, she took her reading glasses out of their case. After checking the telephone number in her notebook, she started to dial her daughter's number in New York.

Soon after that, my cousin must have answered the phone. My aunt spoke her name in a high-pitched voice, and opened her eyes wide, as if she could see my cousin right there in front of her.

My aunt had abruptly announced that she was going to call her daughter. I calculated that it must be seven or eight o'clock in the morning in New York. I told my aunt, "This is probably the busiest time of her day. She has to get her husband off to work." But she wasn't listening. She had already gone to get the telephone.

The sound of the rain and the sound of my aunt's voice speaking her daughter's name collided for a moment and then separated. My aunt was bent over the telephone on the floor, as if to embrace it. The sound of the rain and her voice echoed throughout the entire room.

I leaned my back against the cabinet door and stared at the rain streaming down the window. My aunt was right near me— she was so close to me that I could have reached my hand out and touched her face or her back, bent in a curve. But little by little her voice and the sound of the rain grew farther and farther away.

"I like *Ajumŏni*'s voice and *Ŏnni*'s voice. I like the way you two speak Korean. Everything you say flows into my body."

I could hear Yu-Hee's voice from beyond the intermingling of the rain and my aunt's voice, just as though she were walking toward me.

I had noticed Yu-Hee listening attentively to my aunt's telephone conversations many times—not when she was talking to her daughter, but when someone would call her. Yu-Hee might be sitting on the sofa in the parlor, or on a chair in the dining room, or in this living room, but she would listen whenever she was close enough to hear. I also remembered the way she drew near to us, the first day she came to this house, as if we were old friends, and how she listened so closely to our voices as we spoke.

My aunt and I had lived together so long and had heard so much of each other's voices—perhaps it was because my ears had become accustomed, but I had no idea what it was that Yu-Hee found so fascinating about our voices or the Korean we spoke, particularly in the case of my aunt. I was actually embarrassed. But now, listening from a distance, I thought I understood what Yu-Hee had meant. Perhaps the look in a person's eyes, or gestures, or posture, are all part of a person's voice, as Yu-Hee used to say.

"*Ah*," I murmured. I closed my eyes, and then opening them a crack, murmured "*ah*" again, just as Yu-Hee had, one day.

I summoned Yu-Hee's face from within my memory and pictured her bright eyes darting behind her glasses, as though she were right here with me now.

The vision of the mountain flickered before my eyes. The expanse of towering craggy mountain exposed its magnificent rocks and displayed the bold lines of its ridges. Again and again, it advanced and then receded. During this time a huge crevice opened up in one of the rocks at the peak. In an instant the crevice widened. Then the rock broke in two and crumbled into bits.

I started. It felt as though the tiny lump deep in my chest were also breaking in two and crumbling to bits. A dull numbness was coursing through my blood and spreading through my whole body.

My aunt was still talking on the telephone.

She had forgotten that I was there in the room with her. She was still leaning over the telephone, listening attentively to the voice on the other end of the line, as though to keep from missing a single word.

I clasped my bent knees tightly to my chest to collect the fragments, and put the lump together the way it had been. The feeling of numbness disappeared little by little. But I sensed danger—that the lump might split open at any moment—I felt a dull pain deep in my chest.

I closed my eyes, and Yu-Hee was next to me, just as she had been on another occasion, and she seemed to be looking up at me. That day had been a pleasant and happy one, but now it had become a painful memory. With Yu-Hee gone, I could reflect on that day from a fresh point of view, and I realized that the memory could only be painful.

It was at the beginning of this year, around the time when the new semester had started. The two of us had promised my aunt that we would be waiting for her when she came down from the mountain, where the path began. We were going to meet her there when she returned with the medicinal water she always brought down from the mountain, and then walk home with her. Since neither Yu-Hee nor I went out very much, my aunt, who wanted us to get out and get some exercise, came up with this idea.

"What is the matter with you two young women? Mountain-climbing is so good for your health! Seoul is a wonderful city.

You can go mountain-climbing any time. I don't understand the young people in Seoul—what's wrong with them? What a shame!"

This is what she had said, smiling, when the two of us declined to climb with her, and then she left the house early in the morning.

Then it was decided that Yu-Hee and I would go out—we would leave early and take a leisurely walk to where the path up the mountain began.

We walked up the hilly road in front of the house, in the opposite direction from our usual paths. When that road veered to the right, we took the road that ran downhill, in front of us and to our left. At the bottom of the hill we came out onto a wide road. There was a tunnel on the other side of the road.

We crossed the road, and began walking uphill. Yu-Hee said that this was the first time she had been here. When we had walked a little up the gently sloping road, there were no more houses. A wide expanse of woods stretched out on both sides, and a brook ran along the left side. The two of us walked slowly, near the railing.

The mountain soared in front of us. Its bold, rugged lines rose strikingly beneath the sky, and its base stretched out as far as you could see.

The road was fairly wide. Once in a while a taxi would approach from behind, drive past us, and then disappear. On a rise in front of us, to our left, was a row of European-style houses. We could see their roofs above the treetops. Except for the occasional noise made by the taxis, there was no sound. There were no people around. Other than the singing of birds and the sound of the water flowing in the brook, there was only silence.

"If you go all the way up to the top, there's a monastery up there on the left, deep in the woods."

I pointed it out to Yu-Hee, who was walking beside me.

"I can't believe there's a place like this in Seoul! *Ŏnni*, Big Sister, this is part of Seoul, isn't it?"

I smiled at Yu-Hee, and nodded.

Yu-Hee had said that she didn't want to climb the mountain, but she had agreed to walk as far as the base. She was in a good mood and seemed contented. So much so that when I looked at her then, I had trouble remembering the strained, gloomy expression on her face, or her hesitant speech, when I would see her in her room at night.

"Yu-Hee, you're always saying how beautiful the mountain is. It's stately and powerful, and if you look at it closely, you feel sad."

"You're right, *Ŏnni*."

Yu-Hee looked straight ahead, and after a little while, she gazed leisurely at the contours of the ridges, and then looked away.

"Each rock has its own expression. Don't you think so, *Ŏnni?*"

"Yes, I was just thinking the same thing."

It was such a beautiful day.

There was no wind, and the morning sunlight was gentle. The color of the rock surfaces, the blue of the sky, all the scenery that filled our eyes, was serene and clear.

Yu-Hee suddenly burst into laughter. I turned to look at her.

"*Ŏnni*, I think that Seoul's rocky mountain symbolizes Korea and the Korean people."

She was trying not to laugh. I asked her what she meant.

"Because they're all naked like the rocks. They don't have anything on. They're always exposed."

She held her hand on her mouth to keep herself from laughing at her own words.

"Well . . ."

I was more pleased to see Yu-Hee laughing than amused by what she had said.

We stood together by the railing and watched the water running in the brook. Yu-Hee's face was cheerful and serene. She had been bent over the railing in silence, but now lifted her head and looked up at me.

"*Ŏnni?*"

"Yes?"

"What is the first thing you think about when you wake up in the morning?"

I couldn't think of an answer right away, so I turned the question back to Yu-Hee.

"What do you think about?"

I was also eager to know what her answer would be.

"I said 'think,' but what I meant isn't exactly thinking."

Yu-Hee suddenly became silent. She seemed hesitant about continuing. After a bit, she started to speak again.

"I don't know exactly how to describe it. I can never remember, when I wake up, if I've just been dreaming, or what I've been thinking about. But I . . . I make a sound. Do I really mean that? I don't know if I should call it a sound. I might just be breathing."

"What do you mean?"

"Well, it's not a distinct sound like *ah,* and it's not as long as *ah,* but a sound comes out of my mouth."

I laughed at this totally unexpected reply. Yu-Hee, too, laughed as she said, "Yes, *Ŏnni*, it's funny, isn't it?"

Yu-Hee moved away from the railing and turned to face me. The expression on her face had returned to its usual seriousness. She closed her eyes, then opened them just a bit, and said "Ah," in a small voice. "No, that's not it," she murmured to herself. Again, she closed her eyes, and repeated the same process.

Now silent, Yu-Hee shifted her gaze in the direction of the brook. I could sense that words that weren't really words were writhing in her mouth.

"It's my 'word crutch'.

"I think I'm trying to see if I can grab hold of my word crutch the moment I wake up."

I didn't say anything.

"It depends on whether it's the Korean *ah* or the Japanese *ah*. If it's the Korean *ah*, then I would have the crutch which continues *ya, ŏ, yŏ*. If it's the Japanese *ah*, that crutch goes on, *i, u, e, o*. But there hasn't been a single day when I was sure which one it was. This has been going on for a long time. And the longer it goes on, the more confused I get. I can't grab hold of the crutch."

Yu-Hee had spoken of her "word crutch," but what she described was a "crutch made of words."

I remembered her voice as she spoke then, which still seemed as distinct now, and the expression on her face.

As the memory faded, my aunt's voice gradually seemed closer, and together with the sound of the rain beating on the windows, it penetrated my ears and reverberated.

I stood up. The telephone conversation continued, with no sign of ending.

I started walking. My aunt didn't seem to notice that I had left the living room.

I stood behind the sofa in the parlor, and touched the back of it with my fingertips. I traced lines with my fingertips, experiencing the sensation of the plush material, and slowly dug my fingers deep into the sofa.

I intended to go upstairs to look at the sheaf of papers that Yu-Hee had left behind. I was fascinated by the spell of Yu-Hee's writing. It was as if someone had summoned me—I was pulled out of the living room.

But for a while I just stood still, looking out at the rain and wind blowing around in the dark garden. I breathed a deep, heavy sigh.

"She's not in this country anymore. She isn't anywhere."

My murmured lament sank into my chest and spread out. The tiny lump quivered slightly.

A strange numbness attacked my feet, my hands, my chest—my entire body. My sighs were contorted by the numbness, and my breathing became uneven.

I turned around and stood facing the staircase. My steps were unsteady, and I felt dizzy, as if I couldn't get my balance.

The tiny lump quivered and burst, and Yu-Hee's face appeared before me.

I blinked slowly, and murmured, "*Ah.*"

Then Yu-Hee's writing appeared. The Korean letters that she had written drifted in front of me, superimposed on her Japanese writing.

I couldn't move. It was as if my crutch had been snatched away. I stood there, paralyzed, at the foot of the stairs. Yu-Hee's two kinds of calligraphy had become fine needles, and were piercing my eyes. I felt the sharp points of the needles penetrating deep into my eyeballs.

I couldn't go on. The vowel *ah* stuck in my throat—the vowels which follow *ah* just wouldn't come out.

Translated by Constance Prener

ON A MOONLESS NIGHT

Sei Takekawa

BORN IN TOKYO, SEI TAKEKAWA WAS A STUDENT AT AOYAMA UNIVERSITY, WHERE SHE MAJORED IN THE ANCIENT HISTORY OF THE WEST, SPECIALIZING IN THE RELIGIONS OF THE ROMAN EMPIRE. SOME OF THE WRITERS WHO HAVE INFLUENCED HER WORK ARE JUNICHIRO TANIZAKI, KYOKA IZUMI, URSULA K. LEGUIN, AND MARGUERITE YOURCENAR, AS WELL AS MANY HORROR-STORY AUTHORS. SHE ALSO REPORTS AN INTEREST IN JAPANESE CULTURE, ESPECIALLY TRADITIONAL CUSTOMS, BUDDHISM, AND FOLK HISTORY.

TAKEKAWA'S FIRST BOOK, **SPACE STATION WITH EVIL SPIRIT,** A SCIENCE-FICTION HORROR STORY FOR CHILDREN, WAS PUBLISHED IN 1985. SHE HAS SINCE PUBLISHED THIRTY-FOUR BOOKS OF HORROR AND FANTASY STORIES FOR CHILDREN AND ADULTS.

When I was a little girl, I hated insects. Maybe, though, I shouldn't say that I hated them; I probably mean that I was afraid of them. It didn't matter to me what type of insect it was; it could be a caterpillar, a moth, or a mantis. Bees' nests were what I hated the most. Yeah. It wasn't the bee that flies around buzzing; it was the bee's nest.

I don't know why I'm afraid of bees' nests. Those bees' nests sure are mysterious things, though—all so intricately matted together with mud, made by honeybees or who knows what. There are those baby insects, like maggots, and those bees with their moist and shiny bodies writhing beneath that mud being molded into a sculptured pattern.

Just thinking about it makes my spine tingle. Maybe I shouldn't blame bees' nests for my fear of insects, though.

My mother says that she doesn't remember it, but when I was very little—when I was really just a baby—I was covered with a swarm of bees. That has to be it. The fear was ingrained in me, going to the very root of my consciousness.

As I got older, I gradually started to come to terms with my dislike of insects. Now I think that butterflies and dragonflies are pretty, even cute. That is, unless I see them up close.

Looking at insects up close gives me the creeps. They've got those multiple eyes and those legs that are all knotted. There's their abdomens twitching. . . .

People often say, "You shouldn't look at them if you don't like them." People who say that kind of stuff don't understand human nature.

My eyes focus right in even as I tell myself, "Don't look! Don't look!"

I'm coming to terms with my hatred of insects, but even now I can't stand bees' nests. Not just bees' nests, but also anything that even looks like a bee's nest. Things that are densely packed or crammed together. Like branches of trees where insects have ceremoniously laid a lot of eggs or trees that bear so much fruit that there is little room for anything else. . . .

Oh, yeah. There are the paintings of Serafine Rue, an artist in the simplistic school. Serafine Rue only paints pictures of flowers, so many in number that they overflow in large vases. There's all these flowers. There are all types. He paints them in as much detail as he can. He doesn't miss a trick. The focus is not in any one place; it's everywhere. He pours the same energy into every flower.

On a Moonless Night

A friend of mine loaned me a collection of his paintings. Looking at them sent chills up my spine. No. Maybe that's not right. Not exactly chills. I felt like a caterpillar was crawling up my spine.

There I was. My eyes were glued to those pictures.

I could see every detail of the flowers. Every wrinkle or line in the petals, stamens weighted down with pollen, calyxes, stems that seemed as though tiny, fine shreds of fur were growing off of them.

How can flowers be so grotesque!

My friend, who had lent them to me, asked in amazement, "Why are you shaking?"

I just stared into that collection of paintings as if I were ready to gobble them up.

When I got hold of myself, I realized that I had broken out into a cold sweat all over and was trembling.

It seems that all of my friends have found out about my weakness. Some of them like to play practical jokes on me. Sometimes they will show me strange things to get a reaction out of me.

One of them gave me a bouquet of purple flowers called ginjiums. Those flowers looked like blossoms from Welsh onions that had been enlarged. There was another time that a friend took me to see a picture that had been created from rice.

There is nothing unusual about rice in bags. But when I saw kernels of rice carefully arranged and all stuck together, I felt claustrophobic. It was strange.

Fortunately, the people that I work with don't seem to know yet about my fears. I've been working at that company since I graduated from junior college two years ago. It's a producer of pet foods. It's a small company, but with so many people wanting to have pets these days, business is good.

I'm in the Planning and Development Section. In our division we are supposed to come up with new foods and toys that cats and dogs will like. We often go to various pet shops in Tokyo and do market research on our ideas.

Although I don't like insects, I do like animals. So my boss feels that I am well suited for the job.

The end of September. . . .

There was no moon that night.

It might have been because there were some clouds; yet I doubt that the moon would have been visible even if it had been clear.

It must have been a new moon, though.

I left the Planning and Development Section about ten o'clock.

We were preparing to present a plan for new products that were coming up. So all of us in the Planning and Development department had been working a lot of overtime.

Since I was a young woman, however, I got to leave a bit earlier than the rest.

I say "the rest." Actually, there were only four other people in the section.

The moon and the stars were hidden by a thin veil of clouds, but it was a pleasant evening, and there was hardly any humidity. The wind, though not strong, almost seemed to stroke my skin as I walked along; it felt nice.

The company was located in Nakano, a section of Tokyo. I lived near Shimokitazawa, so I changed trains at Shinjuku, the main business district on the west side of town.

The area around Shimokitazawa tends to be a quiet residential neighborhood, and on weekends I usually go to Shimokitazawa. I like my living situation.

I live in an elevator building. Some people might think that that is more prestigious than living in, say, a smaller apartment house. Don't ask me why, though. My apartment is just a studio.

I can't afford any more than ¥70,000 per month for rent. My parents do still provide me with a small allowance, really little more than pocket money, and I can afford to spend money on clothes and other things.

I wouldn't want to do anything like take a part-time job in a bar. . . .

It takes about twelve, maybe thirteen, minutes to get from the train station to my apartment.

It was just around ten-thirty. There had been a lot of people around the station, but once I reached the residential part of the area, I didn't see a soul.

In the daytime, though, it would not have been odd for there to have been many people about there.

It was quiet, but in almost all the homes the lights were still on, and I could hear the sounds of televisions and radios in the background.

It wasn't hot, yet it wasn't cold either. Just a pleasant temperature, really, on a moonless night. . . .

I knew the street. I'd been walking it for the past year and a half at that same pace every day, going home.

I had already eaten dinner. I had had a pizza with the people from work. "When I get home, I'm going to have a typical Japanese snack," I had said to myself.

Pizza always seems dry to me, something that sort of sticks in the throat. It's hard for me to eat a lot of pizza at one sitting. It's the cheese too. It seems to just sit in my stomach, like a lump.

"I'm certainly very Japanese," I thought.

I started to mull over what I had in my small refrigerator. "There must be some pickled radishes or salted eggplant. I know that I didn't eat all that fish. There's other things too, I'm sure."

I always keep in some packaged instant rice that I can fix when I get hungry for something. What could be worse than coming home tired, wanting something to snack on, and finding that you don't even have rice?

"Huh!"

I stopped in my tracks.

"Huh!" Something was dropping on me. No, it wasn't exactly like something dropping, it was more like something was falling on me.

But these were too big to be raindrops.

"Huh!" Something fairly big had fallen right into my open palm when I was trying to find out what this was all about.

It was about seven or eight centimeters long. It was a thin, long thing that had to be at least a centimeter wide. It was green.

"Echh!" I guess I just stared at it for a few moments, then I tossed it away. I gave my hand a good shake. It was a caterpillar.

"Echh!"

I let out a yell and ran into the center of the street, then I looked up.

There was a big tree.

It was probably a cherry tree. It was in the garden of what appeared to be the home of some fairly well-off family. Its branches extended out majestically.

"That must have dropped from the tree." But there sure were a lot of those things dropping.

I had to wonder whether the tree was breeding a bunch of harmful insects. I mean, there weren't just one or two insects that had dropped; there were a lot. At my feet, in the light of the street lamps, I saw a large number of them, all scattered around and crawling about.

I cringed in fear. I was paralyzed for a moment.

Insects . . . a big bunch of them. What I hated the most.

The hair on my back was standing on end. I could feel the cold sweat flowing down my chest.

"Echh!"

I screamed again, as if that would bring me back to my senses. I buried my face in both hands, held my breath, and fled.

Ecch. That feeling, the one that you sense when you step on something soft. I could sense it there on the soles of my feet. It seemed to penetrate through the pumps that I was wearing.

I slipped and almost fell down. Yet, somehow, I kept my balance.

I don't know how many meters I ran without stopping.

I finally stopped, caught my breath, and stamped my foot in disgust.

"What is this? Why me? What did I ever do to deserve this?"

I don't know how many times I scraped the soles of my shoes on the asphalt pavement. The body juices from the insects had stuck to the bottoms of my shoes.

I wondered what color a caterpillar's insides were. I thought that they must surely be a sickening green.

"Go home. Right now. And take a shower," I kept saying to myself, and I started walking again.

I had made up my mind to forget all about what had happened, and the sooner, the better.

"Sure, I'll hurry home. There's some snacks waiting." I quickened my pace.

"But . . . one of those snacks is roe. If you look close, roe is like a bunch of tiny granules all packed together."

That reminded me of what I had just gone through.

"I suppose I won't be able to eat roe for some time. From now on, whenever I look at roe, it'll remind me of what it felt like stepping on and smashing those caterpillars."

Memory is a mysterious thing. It is set off by something. Maybe a place or setting, a smell, something to eat. . . .

There could be a fig tree in a garden. When you pick the unripened fruit, out comes white juice. Whenever I eat a fig, I always remember that white juice. Then I never fail to recall Ryo, my macaw. His feathers and the smell of his droppings come back to me clearly.

Ryo used to like to peck at unripened figs.

For me, for Ryo too, it was only a game.

There was a fig tree growing in a garden, ever so small. Without fail, that tree bore fruit every year, but the figs were never large enough to eat.

That white juice smelled like fish.

Figs are full of little granules, too.

"Stop it!" I thought.

It seemed like everything was getting to me.

I looked up at the sky.

There was no moon, and there were no stars.

The sky was veiled in a thin coat of clouds.

"What is it with today . . . ?"

"In just two or three more minutes I'll be home. I'll feel better then."

My home. It may be small and messy, but it is still my castle.

A moonless night makes you feel bad, for some reason. Even the smell of the air is heavy and humid.

Suddenly I felt that the sky had become cloudy, cloudier than it had been before, I sensed. But I couldn't bring myself to look up at the sky.

There was a person standing in front of me. Insects frighten me, and so do strangers. Murder, rape—well I shouldn't go that far, but a purse-snatching could happen even in an area that is considered very safe.

I clutched my shoulder bag even tighter.

I tried to walk around him. I went to the right side of the street, and as soon as I did that, he moved in the same direction. I went left. He went left. I tried to convince myself that there was nothing to worry about.

We each tried to avoid the other but ended up moving in the same direction and ran into each other. "Pardon me," I said. "Bad timing." He didn't say anything, though. Usually that kind of attitude would have irritated me, but that night I just couldn't be bothered.

There was something about him that made me apprehensive. He was tall and seemed to have a good build. I assumed, and I had been assuming, that he was a man. But, there was something peculiar.

I don't know, but there had been something strange about him from the very start.

He was wearing a crumpled raincoat. "It's always better to let sleeping dogs lie," I reminded myself. I stopped where I was and waited for him to pass. He came right up in front of me, however. It dawned on me finally. I didn't hear footsteps. None.

And there was something about the way he walked. . . .

Should I call it "walking"? No, it was more like he was side-stepping. It was like he had caterpillars stuck to the bottoms of his shoes too.

"I'd like to pass," I said. I had been trying to have nothing to do with him all along, but I saw his face for the first time.

It wasn't a face.

At least, it wasn't the face of a human being.

It was like someone had carefully put a bunch of things together in an effort to construct a human face.

I remembered a picture that I had seen, one in which vegetables and fish had been put together to resemble a human face. This was like that. But, of course, there weren't the vegetables or the fish.

Huh. The face was moving. The face was moving, as though it were in spasms.

"Please. I'd like to pass!"

I tried not to look. I didn't want to look. I couldn't seem to help myself, though; I just stared into that face.

The face had swelled up, the way that a wave does on the sea. The face started to break up. The cheeks, the mouth, the eyes—they were all moving just as they pleased.

I tried to scream, but I couldn't. My whole body was stiff.

The form of that man continued to become more distorted and deformed. His body was breaking up right before my eyes.

Things popped out from the top of his head. No. They didn't pop out. They flew out.

They had wings. They were beetles that were as big as gold bugs. Their bodies were a shiny jet black, as though they had been coated with oil. In unison, they were making all sorts of noise, flying around and about, and then they flew back to where they were, as though they were dancing. They flew all around my head.

Buzz . . . buzz.

A vibrating sound.

I kept staring at the thing that I had thought was a man. His head was completely destroyed. From the sleeves of his raincoat winged insects emerged, one after the other. Thin, long things. Beetles, moths, centipedes, caterpillars, earthworms . . . insects of every type.

I almost fainted.

I was completely dazed. The centipedes and the caterpillars started crawling up my legs.

The raincoat fell to the ground. There was nothing in it. A swarm of insects had been wearing the raincoat.

"This is just a dream!" I said over and over to myself, determined that I had to believe that. If I did, then I would be able to make my legs move. I started moving backward.

"Don't come near me!"

I held my breath and backed away.

It was hard to tell whether the band of insects was actually aware of me. I hoped that they were just there, crawling and moving around.

I soon realized how stupid that hope was.

The swarm of insects quickly decided on one course. My direction.

"What is this . . . ? Insects don't walk around wearing raincoats."

"I don't get it, but there must be somebody who is telling these insects what to do. Is this some mutation . . . ?"

"This just can't be!"

I shook my head. "This is absolute craziness! This just doesn't happen! This has just got to be a dream!"

"Ha. Ha. Ha, Ha. Ha." I was laughing, but really for no reason.

I had certainly had a nightmare in which I found myself covered with insects. How many times had I dreamed it? In that dream, a swarm of insects would cover me and slowly start to devour me. Caterpillars and centipedes there crawling around all over my skin. Nothing was as frightening as that.

I have often dreamed it. When I was a student, somebody once told me, "Your worst and bitterest fear is the mirror image of what you truly desire." He had been a most unusual boy, one who knew something of philosophy and psychology. He used to mention names of people that I had never heard of—Jung or Roland Barthes.

But the things that he said to me have always been somewhere in my mind.

I remember a time, it was during summer vacation, that we all went camping in the mountains.

I had attended a women's junior college, but we often had extracurricular activities with guys attending universities.

That camping trip was one of those times. We didn't use tents. Rather, we rented a bungalow. And when night fell, we all got together and told ghost stories.

After the ghost stories, we started talking about ways to die. I remember there was the question, "What do you think is the most brutal and cruel way to die?"

Everybody gave his thoughts on the subject. There was this girl, she was so obese, and she said, "Dying from starvation." She was one of those fat ones that always seemed to be munching away on something.

"Drowning would be painful. You suffocate." That was the opinion of a boy who liked water sports, and I remember that he said it rather lightheartedly. I suppose that he was quite satisfied and sure of his prowess at swimming.

"Airplane crashes." That was what another girl said. "I don't suppose that you suffer much in an airplane crash. After all, you are killed instantaneously. For that matter, you would probably pass out first prior to the actual crash. But . . . you know . . . your body would be strewn everywhere. I sure don't want to die in an airplane crash."

One after another, everybody told everybody else what they thought would be the worst way to meet your death.

I talked about insects. I mentioned that nightmare, the one that I would always have, dreaming that I was covered with insects and dying that way.

Everybody just sort of gave me a funny look. They must have been thinking that I was pretty strange.

But a boy came to my rescue. That was the guy who liked Jung. I remember he said, "Me, I'm afraid of being eaten by a shark." He wasn't particularly muscular, just average, I guess, and he wasn't especially tall, again average. He was one of those people that you really wouldn't notice in a crowd. He was the type that liked to talk about "serious" things. I wasn't the slightest bit attracted to him, really. But it seems he was interested in me. Somebody told me, "You know, that guy has got it for you."

He never asked me for a date, though.

"I always think about what it would be like to be eaten by a shark."

"Hmm . . . it sounds painful," said one girl.

"When I find a documentary on sharks, I always rent it, take it home, and copy it."

"You're an idiot," said another guy in the group.

"No."

He said that last remark with a very serious face.

The mirror image of what you truly desire. . . .

"You're joking!" I shook my head fervently, as though there

were a swarm of insects right before my eyes and I was trying to shake something filthy from my hair.

"I sure as hell don't have that desire. No. Not at all."

The swarm of insects kept crawling closer to me.

I thought that even if it were a dream, I surely would have tried to flee.

Plunck. Something struck me on the face. It was a flying insect. It felt like someone had put some ice down my back out of nowhere. I felt some pain. I felt my hair, shoulder length, brush against my cheek.

In a dream you don't feel pain or have any sense of touch.

"It can't be true!" Surely someone, somewhere, has had a dream where he did smell something. People might have had dreams about the smell of the seashore, or in their dreams maybe some have smelled curry. . . .

But I never have had.

I took a few steps, backed away, then turned. I ran. I didn't care where; I just ran as fast as I could, and I didn't look behind me. The enemies were the insects. "Surely they won't follow me." I was thinking that, but I didn't have the courage to look behind me. It was awful; I didn't want to look. What if they were coming after me . . . ?

Breathless, I ran. I ran and I didn't know where. But I ran.

Buzz.

That thin, shrill sound mingled with the sound of my heavy breathing. It haunted me with its persistence. *Buzz.* That had to be the sound of wings.

It had to be a beetle. It was near me. For some reason, though, my legs were getting heavy. I was out of breath and my legs tangled.

Buzz.

The sound of wings and an omen. . . .

My legs tangled. All I had been thinking about was what was behind me, and my legs tangled. I fell down face forward.

I didn't feel the pain. No, it wasn't because it was a dream. I didn't feel the pain because I was so terrified. I know that much.

"Stop! Stop!" I got halfway up and looked in the direction that the sounds were coming from. There was a band of beetles accompanied by a swarm of bees. Both groups were enormous.

Every bit of strength that I had had failed me.

"No! No! I can't take it!"

"This isn't my desire. I didn't ask for this. They're attacking me because *they* want to."

"What did I do to you . . . ? I only hate you."

Sure, I've poured water in ant holes. When I've spied bees, I've used insecticides. I've burned branches where caterpillars have reproduced. They were still alive.

But these are things that everybody has done.

I covered my face with my hands and cringed.

I thought that the bees would surely sting me all over. The bees in the swarm were large ones whose potent poison could surely kill you.

After that, I imagined the beetles and the other insects devouring me, as I still lay alive, little by little.

"Mother!"

Something made me think that you were expected to call out for your mother when you were dying.

Buzz.

The sound of wings was loud.

It was coming closer.

I was terrified. "Don't look!" That was what my heart was telling me to do. Yet, there was another voice from within me whispering, "Look and see what is coming." I peeked through my fingers.

A gigantic thing had taken the place of the swarm.

It was a bee.

I thought that it was a nightmare. There couldn't have been a creature like that thing anywhere on the face of the earth.

It was a one-meter-long bee.

It wasn't the creation of a bunch of small bees. It was one living bee.

I looked right at that bee. I refused to be afraid, because I had to believe that it was all a dream. Still it was all so eerie.

Buzz.

The gigantic bee was flapping its wings, but it stood still in midair.

Its eyes were shiny, like metal, and I felt that they were focused right on me. Yet I didn't know for sure where or how insects focus their eyes.

Its huge jaws. The insect's huge jaws. They looked as though they could crush the bones of a human's finger with one bite.

Its antennae were twitching. Its large, round stomach. And on the end of that stomach was its stinger. . . .

I started to inch away on the asphalt.

It was cold. The asphalt was cold. I didn't know whether it was a dream or reality.

What I do know is that I only wanted it all to be over. "This isn't my desire! No! Never!" I screamed.

Buzz.

The bee moved forward slowly as I crept backward. We were level with each other—it hovered two meters from the ground—and it stopped.

I dragged myself along on my palms.

The bee was coming after me. Little by little, the space between us grew smaller.

The bee was still in midair, and it was moving its six legs.

I realized that if it were to come only slightly closer, it would get me.

Scch.

Scch.

My back had struck something hard as I inched backward. It was surely a fence.

The bee's legs were hooked at the ends, and it opened them wide. There was a bunch of bristly hair growing there.

Buzz.

The sound of its wings grew louder all of a sudden.

The stripes on its sides were shiny like licorice candy. My vision was totally consumed with that. The bee's stomach.

Then, right after that, something sharp slit my jacket and skirt. It started biting into my skin.

The bee held me down with its six legs.

Those legs were like saws. . . .

I could hear the sound of holes being dug into my flesh.

I wanted it to stop flapping its wings. The bee started to lie upon me. I rolled onto the pavement.

I wasn't in pain, nor was I frightened.

The overpowering presence of the bee had drained me of emotion. The bee stroked my forehead and throat with its antennae. I could see the spasmodic twitching of its stomach. It was like a coat of armor.

The twitching at its stomach had increased. Something was moving along my stomach as I lay there on my back.

It seemed as though the point of a sharp knife was caressing my body.

I felt a twinge of pain right in the middle of my stomach.

Then there was a sharp pain. It was as though a drill had been rammed into my stomach.

"Ugh . . . !"

I didn't let out a cry; I passed out.

When I awoke, I was in a hospital bed. Someone who had happened to pass by had found me unconscious and lying on the ground.

Everyone thought that I had been attacked and raped.

Yes, they all thought that because I had been lying there on that street with my clothes torn to shreds.

But, the results of the examination showed no indication of rape.

Still, my clothes were torn to pieces, and I had cuts all over my body.

I couldn't speak for a while, either.

The police drew their own conclusions: She was attacked by several people, those persons saw the passerby, and they stopped what they were doing.

I let it go at that too.

Can't you just hear it now—"Well, I was just walking along and there were these insects. . . ." Who would believe it?

The doctors still couldn't fathom that cut on my stomach, though.

I was in the hospital for almost three days.

The cut on my stomach healed much more quickly than usual. The people at the hospital seemed to think that the attackers were deranged.

After I was released from the hospital, I stayed at my parents' home in Chiba, about an hour's train ride from Tokyo, about ten days for convalescence. Then I went back to Tokyo and to the job.

The people that I worked with, though concerned and sympathetic, somehow seemed to look at me as though I were the culprit. I didn't care, though.

I didn't care; I couldn't do anything about it.

Then there was that day that an older woman in the company happened to say, "Have you been eating more than usual lately? I mean, I was wondering whether things might be bothering you and you sort of turned to eating. . . . You know . . . ?"

"Ah. . . . Well. . . . Eating because things are bothering me . . . ?"

"Well, don't you think that you've put on some weight lately? I mean around your stomach."

She said it rather jokingly.

"You always had such a good figure."

"Well, you guessed it. I do have the 'Over-eaters Plague.' Only kidding." I laughed cryptically.

But, yes, it was true. My stomach was bigger. Because inside of my stomach there was a life growing.

The gigantic bee had laid an egg in my womb. Those types of bees do it as a matter of course. They lay eggs inside their prey. The eggs hatch, and the young feed on the insides of the prey, grow, then eat their way to the outside.

Of course, the victim is living all through that.

The egg there in my womb has hatched. I can feel something moving inside my stomach. Sometimes it kicks there inside my womb, and I can feel the pain run through me.

When my sister had been pregnant, she had shown me a picture of the fetus there in her womb, taken by supersonic wave photography techniques that they now use in medical analysis. I remember that it had looked like the larva of a beetle.

I wonder if that is what the thing there inside my womb looks like.

Whenever I feel it move, I am overcome with emotions that I can't explain.

I wonder if it's the love that a mother has for her offspring.

The larva is eating away at the flesh there inside me and will come out.

I know that.

The insect will devour my entire body, and I shall die.

I wonder why it had terrified me so much.

I wonder why I dreamed it so often. Yes, I feel as though I dreamed it every night.

It wasn't the mirror image of what I truly desired.

It was a premonition.

Why have I had that premonition since the day that I was born?

So, there ends the story.

Translated by Mauricio Lorence

LIVING IN A MAZE

Kyoji Kobayashi

KYOJI KOBAYASHI WAS BORN IN 1957 IN NISHINOMIYA-SHI, HYOGO-KEN, AND ATTENDED THE UNIVERSITY OF TOKYO, MAJORING IN AESTHETICS AND ART. IN 1984 THE MONTHLY LITERARY MAGAZINE **KAIEN (STORM PETREL)** AWARDED HIS NOVEL **DENWA OTOKO (THE TELEPHONE MAN)** THE THIRD SHINJIN-BUNGAKU-SHO, OR NEW WRITERS AWARD. THE NEXT YEAR HE WAS NOMINATED FOR THE AKUTAGAWA AWARD FOR HIS NOVEL **SHOSETSU-DEN (THE LEGEND OF A NOVEL)**, AND HIS FIRST MAJOR NOVEL, **ZEUSU GA-DEN SUIBOU-SHI (THE RISE AND FALL OF THE GARDEN OF ZEUS)**, WAS NOMINATED FOR THE FIRST YUKIO MISHIMA AWARD AND THE NOMA LITERARY AWARD. KOBAYASHI'S NEW NOVEL, **SHE CAME IN THROUGH THE BATHROOM WINDOW**, IS CURRENTLY APPEARING SERIALLY IN **KADOKAWA**, A MONTHLY MAGAZINE. THIS STORY IS AN EXCERPT FROM A LONGER STORY OF THE SAME NAME.

Mr. K's Morning Routine

1

If the day is clear and bright, Mr. K gets up at nine o'clock in the morning. That is something that he has done for the past ten years. If it's rainy or gloomy, Mr. K gets up at nine-thirty. That is also something that he has done for the past ten years. As soon as he gets out of bed, before he does anything else, he takes his medicine. That too is a habit that he has kept for a long, long time. For Mr. K, habits are not something that you change. Rather, you continue to add to them. A good example is in taking medicine. In the beginning, Mr. K was taking only necessary medicines, ones that he could not do without. Now that habit has grown, and at Mr. K's bedside there is little room for anything else except medicines. Every morning Mr. K meticulously takes his medicines in the same order and in the same dosages. First, five tablets of ion calcium. Then, three tablets containing something to improve the constitution. Five grains of a health food that contains Vitamin C. Two tablets each of a nutrient for the liver and a substance to prevent skin disease. One Vitamin E capsule. Two times with an inhaler to prevent allergies. Three cc.'s with a syringe.

When that is finished, Mr. K washes his face. (Or rather he strokes his face, as a cat paws at its own.) He brushes his teeth with an electric toothbrush. He puts some spray on his hair, which has become disheveled during his slumber, to make it lie down. (Mr. K's hair when he first gets out of bed is truly something to see. It makes you stop and think, "Yes, the angry Medusa must be just like that!" So if this is your first time to see Mr. K, you are probably wondering why in the world he is so angry.)

That over, he changes his clothes. The season dictates his clothing. (In that clothing wears out, he can't wear the same clothing for ten years. He alters his wardrobe, therefore, when he has to.)

When he has finished dressing, he goes to get his newspaper from the delivery slot. Mr. K is not especially concerned about what is going on in the world. Therefore, his newspaper-reading is over in two or three minutes.

So, Mr. K's morning routine has begun.

2

Absent some unexpected circumstance, Mr. K rides his bicycle every morning. Even if there is but a trace of rain, he puts on his windbreaker, and off he goes. Though he might be sweating from a fever, even a slight fever, he puts on a training jacket over his sweater. He might have a headache, yet he still snugly wears his headband. And off he goes.

He will not take a break.

Once Mr. K is on his bicycle, he rides like the wind. Sometimes like a gale, other times like a gentle breeze. When he is going straight ahead, he goes straight ahead to wherever he is going; when he turns, he turns with a sweeping, swaying motion.

Mr. K doesn't want any of the belongings that he might be carrying with him on his bicycle to go astray. So he likes to ride along roads where there are no traffic lights.

After he is on his bicycle, he decides his destination—he might cycle around here, or perhaps might try to see what is in store over there.

There is no place—not even a back alley—near his house that Mr. K has not been to at least once or twice. Actually, there is not a spot within a ten-kilometer radius of his house that Mr. K does not know inside and out. He's like the local postman who can tell you everything about his personal route. He could ride along with his eyes closed and still be able to tell you just exactly where he was. (Of course, he wouldn't do that.)

But were he to go just outside that ten-kilometer radius, he would be totally lost. Even if he were to go but one meter beyond that ten-kilometer radius, he wouldn't have a clue.

Why? Because Mr. K is riding along and always looking at the distance meter on his bicycle. And when he gets to that point that is ten kilometers away from his house, he runs into, shall we say, an invisible wall and turns back right there.

This unusual habit is strictly kept. Typical. Mr. K has never gone beyond that ten-kilometer radius once in three years. We can say that that ten-kilometer radius from Mr. K's house is the maze that Mr. K has built for himself.

Every few days, he goes to the boundary of that maze (a point that is precisely ten kilometers from his house), acknowledges to himself that he cannot escape from the maze (naturally, if he feels like that, there is no reason to go outside of the ten-kilo-meter radius), and goes home.

Mr. K's Dreams

1

Mr. K's life is generally under control, regulated by the tight maze that he has built around himself. Yet, there is one exception where he has to face something outside that maze. We're talking about dreams.

Mr. K might not deserve it, but there is nothing that he can do about it. And the bad part is that he dreams a lot. (He thinks he does, anyway.) For the most part, his dreams aren't anything special; generally, they are just your run-of-the-mill dreams.

For example, Mr. K dreamed that he was dancing the polka with a St. Bernard (actually, this St. Bernard was a dog that used to live near Mr. K's house. That dog's barking was something that would bother Mr. K). Although Mr. K had never danced the polka in his life, he was dancing quite well with the St. Bernard. The St. Bernard was very impressed, and the two of them seemed to hit it off. A pact of brotherhood was formed.

However, just when you think that everything is going well, something wrong is bound to happen. The two of them started bickering about who drank the brandy that the St. Bernard had hanging around his neck. They got into an argument about it. In the end, though, the misunderstanding was cleared up, and the two went back to dancing.

Then there was this other dream. Mr. K and the Buddha were having a bread-eating contest, and the winner would get to be Buddha. The contest was coming to the wire, and it was just about to be a dead heat. But Mr. K was leading by a head. Eating one more piece of bread would make Mr. K the winner. As luck would have it, though, out of nowhere flew in a gigantic cock-roach and landed right on top of the piece of bread that Mr. K was to eat. While Mr. K was pondering how to deal with this situation, the Buddha overtook him, snatched up that piece of bread and the cockroach too, ate them both, and became the Buddha.

Just these sorts of dreams. Not much in them, just a bunch of nonsense, I guess. (I don't know what Freud would have to say, but basically, dreams and nonsense are about the same things.) Dreams like these are ones that Mr. K can cope with. But there are those dreams that he cannot cope with. Now we are talking about nightmares.

We aren't talking about just your usual nightmares. Nightmares descend upon Mr. K twice per year, and when I say twice per year I mean two full months' worth. May and November. During those months Mr. K has nightmares every night. Rather, he has nightmares all night long. There is no interrupting those nightmares. And during those months he will not, for the life of him, have an ordinary or pleasant dream. It's absolute hell.

Mr. K has a name for that period: Nightmare Months.

Who knows what the reason is for it. Anyway, while he sleeps, his heart pounds and pulsates like the ringing of a fire alarm. How can his heart even take it?

During the Nightmare Months for Mr. K, going to bed is like being asked to perform hard labor. He sweats so much during the night—about one bucket's worth—that by morning he has lost about a kilogram in weight. His slumber is destroyed by the nightmares. I couldn't tell you how many times Mr. K wakes up screaming during the night. Usually, with nightmares, a person wakes up and then realizes that it was all just a dream. You can relax after that. Not Mr. K. When he goes back to sleep, his nightmare continues. For Mr. K, there is no relief in waking up. It's only like a five-minute break in a long mountain climb. You look at what's ahead and think "Oh, no." When he falls asleep again, the nightmare starts right where it left off.

The toll that it takes on him psychologically is more than he can bear. Memories of the nightmares remain with him in the daylight hours. He walks around with a sense of dread. Reality and fiction are almost indistinguishable. He does not have the confidence to do anything. Constructive activities are impossible. Logic and order don't fit into the scheme of things.

If somebody stares at him, Mr. K goes nuts. He'll see a car and grab his head and shrink in terror. He sees a bicycle and takes cover. The sight of a tricycle is enough to cause him to flinch. Anything that can move or be made to move can frighten him. He saw a pencil once and paled; there was a time that he looked at a fish and was stopped dead in his tracks; and what about the day he spied an earthworm and convulsed with fear? The things that he'll say or do can be ridiculous: "Pay back that money that you didn't borrow!" or "What do you mean? Why did you tell me to jump off a cliff?" He will forget important appointments that should have been kept, but maybe wait for three hours or more at train stations for people that he wasn't supposed to meet.

Pretty bad, huh . . . ?

2

Mr. K finally got mad because his very existence was being controlled by nightmares during the Nightmare Months, and he made up his mind to rid himself of these dreadful nightmares one way or another. He thought about how he would do it. The answer was plain and simple: he wouldn't sleep during those two months. That would keep the nightmares in their place. If he did not sleep at all, however, he would go nuts. So, he decided to grab a few winks when he found the time in the daytime. He would not sleep for long periods of time, mind you. If he did, he would still be prey to the nightmares. And luckily for him, time was something that he had plenty of. So he would sleep a bit off and on every hour during the daytime.

Mr. K had declared war on the Nightmare Months and faced the foe head-on.

Mr. K would listen to FEN, the radio station that broadcasts in

English, all through the night and would jot down the words to the tunes that he was listening to. (Just a side note: it was amazing how much Mr. K's listening comprehension of the English language improved because of this strategy.) During the day, he would ride on trains and buses and grab just a few moments of light sleep.

The results were marvelous (more than he bargained for).

The nightmares were swept from Mr. K's slumber. Although Mr. K would have to cope with physical fatigue, that too did him more good than he imagined. Exhaustion caused by the nightmares had been greater than he had expected. To the onlooker, however, Mr. K seemed fine. Mr. K was in good spirits. It was as though he had discovered a new insight into the human race.

However, there were some scary side-effects to the way that Mr. K had been handling the Nightmare Months. Yes, Mr. K had shaken off the nightmares from his sleep, but they came to haunt him in the real world. The occurrence was on the evening of a full moon on the seventh day after the start of Mr. K's plan of action (i.e., no sleeping during the night).

3

On that evening Mr. K was having dinner with a young girl at a German restaurant that was inside of the maze. The girl's name was Kozue Fujishima, and she was a receptionist at the preparatory school where Mr. K worked. Mr. K had asked her out to dinner a number of times before, yet she had always turned him down because of previous engagements: she just wasn't up to it, her mother was ill, there was an interesting program to watch on TV that evening, there were memorial services for the sister-in-law of her father's cousin, she had a stomach ache, she felt lightheaded. . . . But tonight, for some reason or other, the mood had changed, and she readily accepted Mr. K's dinner invitation. Mr. K was on Cloud Nine.

There were no bad omens.

The wine was good, the conversation stimulating, and Kozue's cheeks were pink and rosy. In the shaded light from the lamp, the tone was set. Mr. K felt that he could go as far as events would allow him, and he was filled with high hopes.

Then it happened, when the main course arrived. Mr. K had ordered Wiener schnitzel, and when it was placed in front of him, the Wiener schnitzel quivered as if it were actually alive.

Mr. K rubbed his eyes.

The Wiener schnitzel quivered again as if it were giving Mr. K a sign. Not only that, though, it mooed. Mr. K looked at Kozue. Kozue, however, was simply using her knife and fork as if everything was fine. Mr. K thought that it was surely just his imagination. He picked up his knife and fork again. He thought that if he ate it it probably would not moo or do anything else out of the ordinary. Yet, the Wiener schnitzel mooed again as if to stop Mr. K from doing what he was about to do. Mr. K dropped his knife and fork. Kozue had a puzzled look on her face.

"What's the matter?"

"Didn't you hear something?"

"Huh?"

"Yeah. It sounded like the sound that a cow makes. . . ."

"No. You're all right, aren't you?"

Moo, Moo, Moo. . . . The Wiener schnitzel was standing up on the plate and mooing now. Mr. K quickly tried to put the Wiener schnitzel, which was standing up, back where it had been with his knife and fork. The Wiener schnitzel, up on all fours, held its turf, however. Mr. K was pressing at the Wiener schnitzel with all his might, but the Wiener schnitzel still stubbornly refused to give in. Mr. K gave a solid thrust with his knife to avoid the disgrace of being defeated by a Wiener schnitzel.

The blow spelled a momentary silence. Mr. K came to his senses, and when he did, he realized that he had broken the expensive bone china plate right in two. Wide-eyed, Kozue looked over at Mr. K.

Living in a Maze

"What's the matter? Fighting with your meat . . . ?"

"No. Ah . . . I'm just a bit tired, you know . . . ?"

"When you're tired, do you fight with your food . . . ? You are a strange one."

Kozue gave a bit of a smile, then she started to laugh.

The waiter happened to pass by. Mr. K quickly handed the broken plate to him. The Wiener schnitzel was still quiet.

"Oh, boy," thought Mr. K. "Looks like fatigue has got the better of me. The nightmares are over, though. I lasted through that," he thought.

Mr. K looked over at the waiter's face. There was long, sticky drool hanging from the waiter's mouth. It was like the sticky drool that hangs from a cow's mouth when a cow is chewing its cud. From various tables all around him, Mr. K kept hearing moos. Mr. K's heart was beating so fast it hurt.

"What's wrong? You look terrible."

"No. It's nothing. Really. I'm OK."

Still at a loss for words, Kozue stared at Mr. K and, my God, there was a huge gold ring stuck through her nose.

"This is a dream. Take it easy. Relax. Nothing to worry about. You'll wake up soon. Don't make so much of this. You're not going to die by having dinner with a cow. Relax. This could be good for you; it's a new experience. Think of it as personal edification. Like meditation. Like yoga. T'ai chi. Doing gymnastics, like those exercise programs on the radio. Settle down. Take it easy. Patience. Hang in there. Buck up. You'll be a better person for this. Relax. Relax. Relax," he thought.

Finally, they were through eating. He paid the check, and they left. As soon as they were outside the restaurant, the cold air seemed to make Mr. K feel better. Kozue once again had her charming face. The gigantic ring in her nose had disappeared. Things were back to normal. (So he thought.)

Mr. K took hold of Kozue's shoulder. She didn't resist his touch. (He fancied himself quite the lady's man.)

"Sorry about all that before."

"Yeah, well, I was sort of surprised. I didn't realize you were so tired."

Suddenly something dawned on him.

"I'm fine. But, you know, I wouldn't mind going somewhere to rest a bit. I feel a bit funny. . . ."

He managed to get her to go with him to a hotel.

While Kozue was taking a shower, Mr. K refreshed himself with a beer. He was sure that everything was back to normal. No worries.

Kozue came out from the bathroom. Mr. K embraced her. The bathrobe gave way as she let herself go into his arms. Kozue's body was even more attractive than he had imagined. "What more could I ask for?" he thought. Mr. K brought her over to the bed. He took off his own clothing.

Moo.

Mr. K was startled. He looked at her. Kozue's beautiful naked body lay under him. He thought that the sound was surely his imagination. "Just lack of sleep," he thought. Mr. K buried his face in Kozue's breasts like a little boy who was ashamed of something bad that he had done.

Moo.

He thought he was suffering from the nightmares again. "Slept too long, I guess." So he raised his head. Lying there was the lovely, sweet, head of . . . a cow.

Mr. K rubbed his eyes.

No doubt about it. It was a Holstein cow. Correct behavior would dictate that Mr. K yell out and jump out of bed, but a nightmare has its own way of doing things. And that power would not permit Mr. K to escape.

Mr. K kept right on doing just what he had been doing. (You got it, though it may be hard to believe.) Mr. K closed his eyes and stroked her body. Instead of tender, soft skin, he felt prickly hide. He took hold of her hands. Instead of five limpid, beautiful fingers, there were hard split hoofs. Mr. K tried to put his mouth to her nipples, but all he found were flabby tubelike things. When he sucked at them, he was rewarded with a blast of milk.

Mr. K thought that he was losing his mind. He felt as though his senses were numb. But he thought that even if he were losing his mind, he was still at least aware enough to try to think about this logically. Mr. K timidly opened his eyes. Yeah, his bed partner was a cow. "If I weren't nuts," thought Mr. K, "I would yell out and get the hell out of this place. And if I *were* nuts. . . . Hmmm, yeah: I would yell out, and get the hell out of this place."

Mr. K thought about it, but he could not come to a conclusion. The bad part about it all was that all during this time, Mr. K did not seem to lose any of his sex drive. Although it might not be rational, he just kept right on with you know what. He was transformed into a puppet. Now Mr. K was the very slave to his nightmare.

In what must have been the world's oddest ecstasy, Mr. K performed. . . .

4

Unfortunately, this was just the beginning.

Mr. K did not feel any better about the situation that he was in even after sex was over. You might say that things started getting worse.

Kozue was a cow now and had been a cow all through the affair. Mr. K sat there on the bed, mumbling to himself. Kozue was placidly looking at him with a blank look on her face, and Mr. K did not have the faintest idea how he was going to handle her.

Mr. K thought that perhaps a glass of water would clear his head. He turned on the faucet, and out gushed a healthy flow of slugs! Shocked and repulsed, he quickly dumped his cup full of slugs back into the sink.

The cow turned around and looked at him, got out of bed, and mooed something to him. Mr. K looked into the cow's face in an effort to fathom what the cow was trying to tell him. He did not get much out of the message, though. With a little body language and a lot of imagination, he got it. "Right. She's saying, 'Let's leave.' " He got dressed.

Still, Mr. K thought that all of this was just something temporary. (Or, at least, he was trying to convince himself that all of this was just something temporary.) "Once outside, into the open air, somehow this is all going to be cleared up—some mistake," he thought.

There was a scorpion in his shoe. His muffler changed into an anaconda, and it was getting tighter and tighter around Mr. K's neck. However, undaunted, Mr. K somehow managed to get Kozue, still a cow, out of the hotel.

Once outside, he took a deep breath. That seemed to make Mr. K feel a little better. "Sure, this was all just an illusion." So he thought. He turned around to see what was behind him. Yeah, Kozue was still a cow.

Mr. K haled a taxi. With as much cheer as he could muster, he said, "Good-bye. I sure had a good time today."

He tried to get Kozue into the taxicab. Being a cow, Kozue was unimaginably heavy, but Mr. K, with all his might, pushed and shoved and, by God, he got her into that taxicab.

Mr. K was still at a loss. He thought he had lost his mind once and for all.

Then, trying to get back to normal, he took a road toward places that he had never seen before and where people had never seen him.

"What's the matter? What's the matter?" he kept on thinking to himself. He found himself in what seemed to be a deserted wasteland. "I don't care anymore. I just don't care anymore," he thought. Then he looked behind him. Three or four monkeys were hot on his trail. Fear gave Mr. K the energy that he needed to escape. He turned. With a bound, he fell into a hole. The hole was full of cockroaches. The cockroaches kept getting into his mouth.

A passerby was giving Mr. K a sinister, evil look. Mr. K was ten meters now from his house. Mr. K was in all kinds of pain because his mouth was stuffed full of leaves.

Mr. K escaped into the sanctity of his home.

The interior of his house had changed into a jungle. There was a black panther sleeping on top of his bed. Nothing he could do about it. Mr. K slept on the floor. The strange part was, though, that he did not have a dream that night.

He slept all through the night. Maybe that was why things seemed as though they were back to normal the next day. "Thank God!" Mr. K thought.

But as soon as he arrived for work at the preparatory school, yeah, Kozue was still a cow. She was sitting there at the front desk, mooing away. "That's it. There's nothing I can do about it. It's over. Finished. I give up," he said to himself.

Kozue mooed something to Mr. K. Mr. K pretended that he didn't hear it and kept right on walking. Kozue charged over to where Mr. K was. Mr. K was horrified, stopped in his tracks paralyzed with fear. But Kozue did not seem to mean any harm. She had a handkerchief in her mouth and she just wanted to give it to Mr. K. The handkerchief was dirty and soggy, though. Mr. K said, "Thank you." Kozue let out a loud, long moo. Then, like a choir in harmony, there were loud, long moos coming from all directions. Mr. K fainted away in this symphony of moos.

5

When he came to, Mr. K was lying in a hospital bed.

The first thing he saw when he opened his eyes was the head of a cow peering at him with a concerned look on its face. When Mr. K tried to utter a few words, the head of the cow put a hand gently to his mouth and struck a serene pose.

"You're something, aren't you? You must have really been

working too hard. You seem to have really done it this time, I'd say."

That head of the cow was saying this to him and smiling just a bit. Mr. K knew that this had to be Kozue expressing concern and annoyance all at the same time. This display of honesty coming from Kozue was about the last thing that Mr. K had expected. When he looked over at her, she had regained her human form from the neck down. Mr. K thought about the things that Kozue had been saying to him and, yes, he did feel a little relieved.

After that, there were the drops of medicines fed to him in the tubes on his arms. He fell asleep, and in his dreams he had a reprieve from nightmares.

(This was the only time, before or after, that Mr. K took any pleasure in having a nightmare in his dreams.) The nightmares did continue off and on even after he was in the hospital. But Mr. K really did not think much of it. (As a side note, Kozue really did seem concerned when she realized how much Mr. K had gone through.)

And starting from December, the nightmares did in fact no longer haunt Mr. K.

6

This episode gave Mr. K a chance to reflect quite a bit on "status quo." While he was in the hospital, he jotted down a few thoughts on the subject. And those notes are provided here.

    1. Status quo [or rather, we should say in Mr. K's life, "a maze"] is something that puts your life into focus and perspective.

    2. When you actively do something to disrupt status quo, you are only inviting confusion, or rather tragedy.

    3. The reason is that status quo is something that does not change.

    4. We can make an analogy between status quo and a pen-

dulum. A pendulum doesn't stop swinging. Its movement isn't based upon change, though. Rather, its movement is based upon not being able to change. Status quo also goes on, moment by moment, and the result is that it is merely following a single course. Trying to change status quo is just as stupid as the thought of a pendulum trying to change its movement pattern on its own. No good comes from the effort. (A cow that tries to take on something that it shouldn't might get caught in a harrow.)

5. How does all this pertain to nightmares? Well, nightmares are an important factor in status quo. Trying to do something about them is just like trying to change the course of a pendulum's movement. The effort is a waste and, at the same time, the more you fiddle with the movement of a pendulum, the more dangerous your deed.

And so, nightmares, no—dreams in general—have a place in Mr. K's life, even though they may not be right inside the maze.

(An afterword: The relationship between Mr. K and Kozue continued for a while. Believe it or not, Kozue was the one that showed the most interest in the affair. Mr. K, on the other hand, quickly started to lose interest in her. It was inevitable that the two would have to go their separate ways. After all, Mr. K was well aware of what Kozue had been like as a cow, and in the flesh she just didn't seem to have that same charisma.)

Translated by David Hanna

THE IMITATION OF LEIBNIZ

Genichiro Takahashi

GENICHIRO TAKAHASHI WAS BORN IN HIROSHIMA IN 1951. HIS STORY "SAYONARA GANG-TACHI" ("GOOD-BYE GANGS") WAS GIVEN THE FOURTH GUNZO NEW WRITERS AWARD FOR LONG STORIES IN 1981. HIS OTHER MAJOR WORKS INCLUDE **NIJI-NO KANATA-NI (OVER THE RAINBOW)**, AND HE HAS TRANSLATED SEVERAL BOOKS FROM ENGLISH TO JAPANESE, AMONG THEM JAY MCINERNEY'S **BRIGHT LIGHTS, BIG CITY,** PUBLISHED BY SHINCHO-SHA. TAKAHASHI HAS ALSO RECEIVED THE YUKIO MISHIMA AWARD.

I may be in some kind of a slump. I must be, because everyone says so. Starting off this season, I made no hits for twenty-seven times at bat (I had nine walks and was hit by a pitched ball once, all of which were caused by the pitchers, who were afraid of me), had an infield hit (this was probably the mistake of an official scorer; or maybe he "gave" me a hit because he felt so sorry for me), and then another streak of no hits for twenty-nine times at bat. By then, the pitchers of other teams in the league knew I was in trouble and started throwing balls smack in the middle of the strike zone. I earned only three walks during that period. Then I had a lucky hit, a grounder which made an irregular bound, and a two-base hit which was caused by a center fielder who made an error in judging the way the ball was going, after which I went no hits for thirty-three (yes, I had one walk). This means I went three for seventy-six, which made a batting average of .0395 (with two sacrifices). In the history of professional baseball, no cleanup hitter has ever had such a low batting average a month after the start of a season.

"It doesn't make sense at all," says the batting coach, leaning on the bat as if it was a cane, "because you hit three-seventy last year."

"It was three-seven-seventeen to be exact. I went one-sixty-eight for four hundred and fifty-two times at bat," I corrected.

"Right. And, you hit three-fifty the year before last."

"Well, I made one-fifty-four for four-thirty-nine, or an average of three-five-o-eight, to be exact."

Three years ago, I went 170 for 447 or .3803. Four years ago, 164 for 460 or .3565. Five years ago, 169 for 470 or .3595. In other words, 824 for 2,268 or an average of .3638, including 205 home runs, 61 three-base hits, 166 two-base hits, and 393 single hits. What do all these numbers add up to? It means that I am a super hitter. If I go 125 for 424, or a batting average of .2948, I am a not-so-bad batter. But if I went only 104 for 420, or a batting average of .2476, I should be either very good at fielding or hit more than 25 home runs; otherwise, I would be a benchwarmer sooner or later. I was a leading hitter four times during the past five years, including a home-run king once and a R.B.I. king twice. The only season I didn't make leading hitter was when, three years ago, although I made the best score in my life hitting .3803, a guy from a low-ranking team snatched the leading-hitter title from me by hitting 12 infield hits in the last ten games of the season, totaling 193 hits for 507 times at bat with a batting average of .3807, while our team was busy clinching the championship. It's really amazing that 41 of his 193 hits were infield hits. Clearly, I was conned.

"You were truly a great hitter," the coach said it in the past tense. "Your batting *was* an art. At least, it seemed that way to me. The manager said he thought so, too. How you could hit like that, we used to wonder. Then what? What the hell has happened to you?"

The very first time I was at bat this season, I struck out. I let all three strikes breeze by. They were as nice and sweet as birthday presents.

"That was the first time I thought there was something wrong with you. Your bat didn't even move a fraction of an inch. You weren't looking at the ball at all, were you?"

But I was seeing the ball pretty well, like seeing a big advertisement balloon.

A good batter is supposed to see the ball a little larger every season. When I first joined the team, the ball the pitcher hurled at me looked as small as a ball in a pinball machine. The pitcher wound up. I concentrated on his hands. *Swish!* . . . and the ball was in the catcher's mitt before I knew it. How could I hit a ball as tiny and fast moving as that? That's the typical question a batter who just became a professional ball-player has. But the pinball-machine ball became a ping-pong ball, a golf ball, an apple, a volleyball, and a watermelon. At the same time, the speed of the ball reduces. From the speed of a rocket, to the speed of a jet, a propeller-driven airplane, a biplane . . . rolling down the steps of civilization . . . finally to the speed of a bicycle in a summer vacationland, and before you know it you will be walking, leaving the bicycle behind. Simultaneous minimization and maximization. And that's what you really want. It's all up to you how to handle a ball that is hanging in the air exactly twenty centimeters off home base, looking like a huge globe. If the ball is a straight ball, it should have a vertical spin, and you should be able to see that it is carrying a foglike ring in a vertical plane, like Uranus, not like Saturn. If it is a slider, it appears substantially different depending on how the pitcher gripped it when he pitched it. The ball should have something white flickering in the center of it if

The Imitation of Leibniz

it was thrown without the fingers' touching the seam, but for some reason I don't know, it should have a red spot in the center if it was thrown with the fingers hooked on the seam. That red spot looks slightly different depending on the pitcher as well as on his condition. If a guy who normally hurls a slider with a red spot as bright as a rose throws a ball which looks like cranberry juice one day, it is a sure sign that he isn't doing well with his girlfriend. However, a guy has to be a .340 hitter constantly to be able to see the ball this close, and there can't be more than ten of them with the two leagues combined. That's why the conversation in the dugout normally goes like, "How was it?" "That slider was reddish-brown. It didn't have enough spin to be carried all the way out to the stand without giving a little top spin to it." "Thanks. I owe you one!" To give it a top spin, you have to hit a ball which is traveling in a corkscrew motion at the speed of 138 kilometers approximately 8 millimeters above the center. Most of the guys just hit the balls with very vague ideas, and that's not batting. Of course, I'm not in a mood to big-mouth like that right now with the condition I am in.

"I think it is just a matter of feeling. You must have lost the knack of feeling because of some very minor incident. How about a thousand swings every day? Wear out your body completely. When your feeling is not ticking properly, you tend to think this way or that, and it just aggravates the situation. But your body still remembers the right swing."

"A matter of feeling," is this coach's favorite phrase. Anything that he can't place his fingers on, he calls "a matter of feeling." He went 2,033 for 7,655, or a lifetime batting average of .2656 during twenty-two years of his career as a player. The only thing he can talk about is how long he lasted as an active player. This batting coach's biggest problem (who wasn't even a regular player during the last four years of his career) is the fact that he never quite understood what batting is. Although he scored more than two thousand hits, he never understood why he was able to do it. Well, it's not such a rare case.

"Try a batting machine," says the coach, "and try to hit the ball with a blank mind. Hit through the center of the ball."

I nodded, went into a batting cage, and signaled to the farm-team coach who was operating the batting machine.

"Keep your arms close to your body. Always check the basics when you are in a slump. Don't open the shoulder. Bring your bat straight down, and hit the ball from above. Hard!"

"OK!"

Of course, I always ignore any advice the coach gives me. If I keep my arms tight to the sides, I would not be able to reach most of the strike zone. If I hit the ball downward, I would get nothing but grounders. I slowly got into a hitting position to wait for a ball. "What are you waiting for?" yelled the coach from the outside of the cage.

"Looking at the balls."

"Twelve balls in a row? What good does it do to you to watch the balls from the batting machine so closely? I told you to hit, didn't I? Is anything interesting written on the ball?"

"Sorry, coach!"

To tell you the truth, there are so many interesting things written on the balls. It is the batter's job to read those things. The machine I am faced with was supposed to be a straight-ball machine, but the balls it was hurling at me had a swirl about ten degrees off the latitude from where it was supposed to be (maybe I should say "longitude," as Uranus is lying on its side), at about where Singapore is, instead of appearing in the center of the vertical fog. I almost felt like I was looking at a photograph of a typhoon taken by a meteorological satellite. If it was off another five degrees, the ball would have curved a little. It probably was caused by a slightly loose screw on the machine's arm. Normally, the more the swirl goes northward, the more the ball curves. An average curve ball has a swirl at the north pole, while some pitchers can generate a swirl on the backside of the ball. It is tough to hit such a ball. In other cases, the swirl on the north pole can come down south and extends like a rain front in the rainy season. Some of the .340-club members claim that this rain front has a double spiral just like a DNA molecule, and that the genetic symbol which constitutes this double spiral has the pitching pattern of the pitcher written on it, but I cannot read it that far. Maybe my ball-selection capability is still far from perfect. In any case, you have to be careful when this rain front appears, because it comes curving down wobbling a little. I always try to hit the center of the ball in such a case. A poor batter always tries to hit the center that he can not see, and doesn't know that the ball can not be controlled unless you hit it a little off center. But if it is a knuckle ball, I hit right into the center. Then the ball goes off the center and comes right to the bat by itself. The rain front is a telltale sign of a knuckle ball. But in some cases, of course, we hit a knuckle ball back. We hit the ball right in front of a fielder and let it bound irregularly. It's a kind of a trick shot, but it is a perfect shot in a case when we want to earn a point during a close game. It took me five years to complete this technique. Of course a straight ball is the easiest to hit, but the crux of the matter is to hit the core of the core of the ball hard (it is an imaginary core with a diameter of about two millimeters in the center of the cork center of the ball) with the core of a bat. What you have to know is that there are only two hit points in the bat. If you hit it that way, the ball flies without any rotation and drops sharply in front of the second baseman or shortstop. There are only about three infielders in the whole league who can catch this kind of ball. Those guys watch balls just before the balls are sucked into their gloves. They are great! Anyway, wait until the balls come close enough to be able to see today's weather. When it comes to within about six meters, we will be able to see the weather. If you want to do good batting, you should wait until the ball comes within 130 centimeters from your body. All the guys of the .340 club do so. I prefer to wait until it comes to within 90 centimeters. If the ball comes closer than that, the pattern on the ball becomes very complicated all of a sudden. Then it is no good. There will be too many things to decipher and no time to swing the bat. You might say that you are too entangled in the thing. When I was a leading hitter, I was called out once or twice a month doing exactly that. "Don't look at the ball too closely," a great slugger I admired gave me advice in a whisper. He was a switch hitter who made the leading hitter of the league six times and in his lifetime batted an average of .367. He was already the cleanup hitter when I was in grade school. He hit 101 hits in the right batter's box and 103 hits in the left batter's box the year he became the oldest leading hitter ever at the age of forty-two. A batter of his caliber doesn't follow the dogma of getting into the right batter's box against a right-handed pitcher and the left batter's box against a southpaw. "I choose whichever box I would like at the whim of the moment. I was originally a right-handed hitter who was forced to practice left-handed hitting with the notion that the left hand is advantageous. In those days, I couldn't walk straight, nor could I understand what I was reading when I came out of batting practice each day. But the coach praised me. He said it was proof that something was being re-structured in my head. I used to be told that I really changed as a person since I became a switch hitter. That was about the time I divorced my first wife. She told me that she felt from time to time that she was dealing with a complete stranger. It was prob-ably that my left-handed ego was beginning to assert itself. I was going through a terrible time. I thought I was losing my identity. That was about the time I divorced the second wife. It was about ten years after I turned into a switch hitter that I was finally out of this ripping torture between the right-handed self and the left-handed self. As a result, when I was at my best as a batter, I was able to see the ball until the last moment of hitting almost as clearly as looking at a global map. But that was only self-complacency. If you want to be really good at batting, you must know your limit. It is not recommended to get into everything." Therefore, although I let the ball come as close as ninety centimeters before I hit it, I no longer watch it closely at that distance. I don't want to be distracted too much.

"All right. It is certainly important to watch the ball carefully, but what you are doing is too much. Do you know how many times you swung your bat at the ball in the last three games?"

"Three times, coach." I confess nonchalantly.

"Yeah, that's once a game. All twelve times at bat, you were counted out. No players in the U.S. major leagues were able to carry a ball without touching it at all, you know. You obviously have a terrific idea in your head. You may be thinking that it is not to your advantage to try to bat with bad swings and prolong the slump. But that kind of negativism will not help you in bringing you out of the slump. Batting is not that complicated. When you are batting fine, you don't have to think about how to make a hit. Here comes a pitch. Whack! Here comes another pitch. Whack! 'Whack' is interpreted as the 'guts,' and that's what you need! Now forget about everything and hit the goddamn balls. Keep your head empty."

But whoever can keep the head empty is the guy who didn't have anything in the head to start with. Why does this guy keep saying "keep the head empty?"

"Keep your head empty, darling." That's exactly what my wife keeps saying. Do all batting coaches think the same way?

"Keep your head empty, darling. You have to relax. Relax. Relax." As she says this, she is clinging to my naked lower body and she is holding my bat in her hand, while I am in a slump of another kind. Yes, she is seriously trying to save me from a slump, wearing negligees and baby dolls of various fancy colors, and playing all kinds of good techniques on me which she learned from women's magazines, night after night. "Do you feel, darling?" Of course I can feel what's being done to my bat. "You feel on the balls too, don't you darling?" "Yeah, yeah, I feel it. I go up fairly high, but . . . this is enough. You must be tired, honey. Why don't we call it a game for tonight, huh? I've got an extra batting training tomorrow morning, you know. I've got to get some sleep." With an ambiguous smile I make a proposal. "No!" She smiles in the semidarkness. "Curing your slump comes first, don't you know?" If it is really a slump, it can be cured. But my bat is not necessarily in a slump. Because when I am with my secret girlfriend, my bat can always whack at it. "Oooh." Groans my wife. "Aaaaaaaaaaaaah!" *Men can also be excited by women's voices (excitation by hearing). Therefore, be free to cry out while you are caressing his penis. Question: How can I cry out while I am doing fellatio? Answer: You may wish to cry out from your deep throat, or you may wish to let his penis go and cry out.* "Aaaaaaaaaaaah!" My wife's groan goes fortissimo. Coach, coach, please leave me alone. This is a slump, and you can't do a thing about it.

"Don't open your shoulder too soon!" the coach roars. "Form a wall on your right shoulder. All right, let's fix that shoulder first."

Didn't he say that I should keep my head empty? One of the oddest things is that they always say "don't open your shoulder." Who the hell started to say that? Poor rookies pretty soon start swinging in a queer fashion caught in an irresistible great chanting of "don't open the shoulder" by coaches and baseball commentators. However odd it feels to hit in such a way, it must be the right way to bat, because everyone says "don't open the shoulder." Even if you hit the ball out of stadium with your shoulder open, they just say, "How can you hit like that with such bad form."

The balls started going outfield as sharp liners.

"That's it. Don't forget that feeling." The satisfied batting coach leaves the batting cage where I've been practicing. And that's all that matters, because I was hitting with my shoulders closed just for his sake. I've learned that it is the only way to get rid of him.

"How ar'ya?" The ace pitcher of our team comes up to me with a smile.

"Oh, I'm in a slump," says I.

"Really?" says he, rotating his shoulder, which is his favorite pose.

"Three hits in seventy-six times at bat."

"Nonsense. It's just a number. I am deep in a slump although I've earned five wins in a row. I know it. I can easily throw a straight ball as fast as 150 kilometers an hour, and it wouldn't be as much as half-an-inch off from the target. I don't have a throbbing pain in my shoulder, either, as I usually had when I was in bad shape. This never happened to me even from my little-league days. And yet, I am definitely in a slump."

The ace pitcher picked up a ball from the ground.

"This is a ball. At least it looks like one to me. And, throwing and hitting it are basically what a baseball game is for. Right? I thought so. But I don't feel that way anymore. I go up the mound. The umpire declares, 'Play ball!' The batter awaits my pitch in the batter's box. I look at the catcher's sign. I give one menacing look at the batter. The first pitch is a fast slider into the high inside corner and forces him to bend backward. That will teach him who the inside corner belongs to. From then on, it will be my pace. The guy will unconsciously keep his head up. Then comes a fast ball clinching into the low outside corner. The next will be the same ball and the same course, but it will drop at forty centimeters before the base. That should do it. Now a smart guy may step the left foot forward about three centimeters after the first strike in the inside high corner. In other words, he wants to aim at the balls coming in the outside low corner. Not so dumb. But that's just about it. No more. Because I'll pitch him a screwball in the knee area. Then a fast ball in the center high ball zone. Zoom. Simple, isn't it? The head is not just a place to keep a helmet on.

Must use it if you are a professional. Hey, I use it all the time. Anyhow, I used to tremble when I was up on the pitcher's mound. But. . . ." The ace pitcher casts an examining glimpse at a young pitcher who is practicing in the bullpen. He talks to himself.

"That's no way to do it. When he pitches a slider, his glove moves ever so slightly. Although he doesn't realize it, something must be twitching somewhere in his body when he pitches a slider. Unless somebody tells him, he will be a sucker. Well, where was I?"

"You said you used to tremble."

"Right. But I don't tremble anymore on the mound. Not only that, I get the feeling of something cold in my chest these days on the mound. Some miserable feeling. I don't know what, but I feel I am totally disoriented. I don't feel I am participating in the game. Even when I am pitching, I feel like I am in each frame of a pitching-form-analysis picture. I can not relate the pitch to the batter's swing and miss. That old man Kant once said, 'Reason asks with what authority a man assumes that a relation necessarily exists between cause and result,' with which I agree totally. What is he doing? What kind of a game is he playing by twirling around there? I would ask. Of course I wouldn't talk to the coach about it. He is incapable of understanding what I am talking about. He would simply say that I should not think so much. This is something I have to solve myself. That's the reason why I always carry a copy of *Prolegomena* in my hip pocket. I keep winning, although I am in a slump because of the old man, Kant. In other words, while my pure reason is full of doubts, my practical reason is preventing the collapse of my personality. 'Human reason has a special destiny in regard to a certain perception, *i.e.,* it is going to be annoyed by problems which reason can not either deter or answer. It can not deter because these problems are burdened on the reason due to the natural characteristics of the reason itself. It can not answer these problems because they are beyond any human reasoning powers,' says *Critique of Pure Reason,* reading of which, in my view, can be much more helpful than practicing two hundred pitches in the bullpen. Because at least the old man, Kant, understands how I feel."

The ace pitcher stared at a ball in his hand. "This one looks so mysterious. I thought I was controlling it, but it may be controlling me, instead." The ace, holding the ball aloft, has set himself in motion and made a pitch to the back net. The ball zoomed in a straight line, skimming along the ground, hopped about thirty centimeters just before the net, and dropped abruptly.

"Holy mackerel!" I cried. "I can't even touch that kind of a screwball even when I'm in the best condition."

"Probably. But, so what?" said the ace pitcher with a pensive look. "Right now I don't care about the result at all. I only want to understand the reason. Have you ever read Leibniz?"

"No, never."

"Then you should read him. He understands baseball. In his *'New System of the Nature and the Communication of Substances as well as the Union between the Soul and the Body,'* the master Leibniz says, 'Phenomenon is not completely imaginative, but is rather associated with event. However, its eventlike nature is not rooted in phenomenon itself. And yet, it has to originate somewhere. It therefore has to be concluded that it exists in a simple substance.' When I read this it occurred to me that this guy understands baseball. If I am the manager, I will make the master Leibniz our pitching coach. In other words, it shows that there is a simple substance in the baseball. It is the ball. The master Leibniz also studied the ball. 'Theory of Monad [ball],' it is called. 'However, a monad [ball] must have a certain character. If it doesn't have a character, even its existence can not be claimed. Furthermore, if it so happens that if a simple substance had character which was not different from another, we would not be able to recognize any changes that occur in a thing.' Isn't it amazing? I thought all along that balls had some character. Old pros think the same way wherever they are, don't they? 'I also think that everyone agrees to the facts that: all created beings suffer from changes; therefore, a monad [ball] that has been created can not be exempted from changes; above all, such changes occur continuously in the monad [ball]. As a conclusion of the above statement, we see that the natural changes of a monad [ball] come from its internal principle. It is because external causes can not affect the inside of a monad [ball].' Do you understand? A ball changes, or curves, because of its internal principle, according to the master Leibniz. I'm amazed."

"Yes, I'm surprised too."

"Yeah? If I showed a copy of *Theory of Monad* to a young pitcher who just turned into a pro, he wouldn't understand a word of it, and he would probably throw it away. 'A ball curves because of its internal principle? What the heck are you talking about? A ball curves because I control it; I cause it to slide,' he would say. As far as I'm concerned they are all big-headed. They have lost humility. That's no good. 'Is that skimpy slider what you call a screwball?' I would ask them. It's not correct even from the standpoint of physics. The pitcher doesn't make the ball change its course. The pitcher simply provides a chance while the ball curves by itself in relation to the air friction. That's how I got this hint." The ace pitcher closed his eyes and continued his story in a pensive mood.

"I thought about it like this. The reason I got into a slump is because I did not understand the internal principle of the ball. 'When we realize that the slightest thought which we conceive includes so many diversities, we ourselves experience so many diversities in a simple substance. If that is the case, everyone who recognizes soul to be a simple substance should recognize varieties in a monad [ball].' Have I been recognizing varieties in a ball? Unfortunately, no. I might have been under a false impression that I was doing something terrific by earning more than twenty wins a year. Although I was throwing more than ten thousand balls a year, I didn't even try to know about it. 'A monad [ball] can only be either created or destroyed all at once. In other words, it does not come to exist only through creation and cease to exist through extinction.' See, the ball does not die. That's why no matter how many times a foul ball is hit into a stand, the umpire throws me back a ball." The ace pitcher was silent for a while and watched the players on the ground.

"What I need now is a reverent feeling. 'Reverent,' that is. No more than three out of a hundred and eighty-three wins I had were won with reverence. That's what I realized. How conceited I was! I didn't understand at all. No wonder I was forsaken by baseball. I was kicked out of baseball without realizing it. I have to go back into baseball again. Fortunately I have the master Leibniz. The master advises a 'stray-sheep' pitcher like me as follows: 'God is the only primitive entity, in other words, the original simple substance, while all monads [balls], which are created, in other words, the derivatives, are generated moment after moment by God as Its products by continuous emanation of the lightening rays of divinity.' What? 'Continuous emanation of the lightening rays of divinity?' What is it? Is he talking about losing sight of a ball when it gets into the floodlight during a night game? Or is he talking about losing the sight of a ball when it flies directly into the sun? I don't think they have anything to do with 'the divinity' in either case. Then, is he talking about a ball which doesn't rotate, such as a knuckle ball? If so, 'the lightening ray' doesn't make sense at all. Sure, a knuckle ball comes down swaying left and right, but it looks no way like a 'lightening ray.' Does he mean I should throw a bean-ball to the batter's head? Then I guarantee that the batter will see a lightening. But I can't continue to pitch bean-balls. With the first bean-ball, I will get a warning, and with the second one, I will be kicked out of the ballpark. I thought and thought. A baseball player ought to think well. He should be different from a stupid professional wrestler or a sprinter. I thought and thought. Is there anyone who is radiating something in the field? In my opinion, it is the catcher. Catchers are always sending signs, aren't they? I wonder if the master Leibniz wanted to say that we the pitchers should not shake our heads. If that is correct, many things fit into the right places. I used to know several catchers who had 'divinities.' For example, the most I could think about pitching combinations was only up to twenty or thirty pitches, but the catcher, who took care of me during my first season in professional baseball, was thinking about the pitching combination as far as the all-star game of the next season. He used to say, 'Look, kid, balls have continuity. Because you threw a curve ball at that point, you wasted a straight ball, the first ball of the next season. Don't try to use the head if you haven't got one. Just pitch as I tell you to.' Sorry to admit, but he was right. While I was struggling to strike out the batter, he was thinking of the confrontation one month later. When I was confronting a current batter, he was planning how to take care of another batter in a future game. When I nervously went up the mound in the first inning and was leveling the ground, this catcher came up and whispered into my ear, 'We are going to win this game by two to one, so you just have to pitch exactly as I tell you.' As I pitched faithfully following instructions, we actually ended up winning the game exactly the way he predicted. Of course, the catchers these days can think only as well as I can and think of only the game at hand. But we have to treat the catchers carefully. I think so. Without them, who is going to catch the balls? If you want to show the catcher your gratitude, it is not enough not to throw knuckle balls. I will never shake my head to the catcher's signs again, however 'primitive' and 'simple' signs they may be."

The ace pitcher left the ground, and I was alone. He had found his solution, but I hadn't found mine yet. Am I really in a slump? Or am I not in a slump? My psychiatrist told me that I am in a slump, a mental one.

"I can see the ball so well, and yet I don't feel like hitting it. I know I could hit it if I wanted to. But the bat doesn't move. My arms freeze up."

"Excuse me, but what do you call your wife?"

"The catcher."

"That's right. Your wife is a catcher, your family is a team, your son is a bat boy, your son's school is the minor league, and what . . . daytime sex is a day game."

Exactly. When sex is stopped in the middle of the action, as often happens with a middle-aged couple like us, it's called a suspended game; if it is done twice in a row, it's called a doubleheader; if it still doesn't come to an end, it's called a playoff; of course, sometimes the game cannot be played because of rain. A red rain and bad ground condition. A cute girlfriend is a rookie who is at the top of the draftees, one who looks like a fast-ball pitcher but is actually a well-experienced screwball pitcher. I try to steal a base under her, evading the watch of the catcher. Most important is the timing of the start. I have to make sure the catcher doesn't detect my intentions.

"I also use such expressions," my psychiatrist says. "For example, 'touch out' when I miss a train."

"That's not the correct expression," I objected to his incorrect usage of the word before I knew it. "If you miss a train, you can still catch the next train. It shouldn't be called a 'touch out.' "

"You're in too much of a baseball groove."

"But. . . ." I object. "I am a professional baseball player."

"You may be. But your family isn't. Me either. You seem to possess no point of view other than that of the baseball game. I think we should better say that you don't have any point of view at all. You are different from a workaholic office employee who doesn't care about his family. You go out to play a baseball game in the morning and come home in the evening to play another baseball game. And, of course, you are playing baseball games in commuting time too. Your slump is caused by that. You're simply playing too many baseball games. Listen. Your body is crying "No more baseball!" It must be getting nervous. If you want to get out of this slump, you just have to stay away from baseball games sometimes. Wipe baseball out of your brain for a while."

Here we go again: "Keep your head empty." Same as the coach. All right. After all, what else do they know to say?

"That's impossible," I said. "I would rather die. Excuse me, doc, you don't know anything about baseball. You may be a 'psycho' pro, I am a baseball pro. I am not a Sunday player."

"Lie down. Stretch your limbs and close your eyes," said the doctor curtly.

" 'A California orange.' Please tell me whatever comes to your mind hearing the words."

"A screwball in the inner low corner," I said in reflex. "Step in on my right foot and delay the start of the swing to aim it to the right field."

"Never mind that. Next, 'the Ministry of Finance.' "

"A safety squeeze play," I responded, "barely making the first baseline."

"Oolong tea."

"A home run curving around the left foul pole. With a flying distance of ninety-one meters."

"A breast."

"A big breast or a small one?"

"What if it is a big breast?"

"A pinch runner. Nineteen stolen bases and seven failures. Meaning that his success ratio in base stealing was .738. But he was pegged four times on the base. I wouldn't want this kind of runner on the diamond on the ninth inning with our team running one point behind the other team."

"What if it is a small breast?"

"A third-place team with eight games behind the second-place and twenty-eight remaining games. It is leading the fourth-place by five and a half games. The probability is that they will finish the season in third place. Fifty-one wins, forty-four losses, and seven ties, amounting to a winning average of fifty-three-sixty-eight. For the period after the All-Star Games, it won nineteen games, lost seven games, and tied twice, leaving a winning average of seven-thirty-eight. Among the games where they scored first, they had thirty wins, nineteen losses, and three ties, meaning a winning average of sixty-three-thirty-three. For those games where they were two points or more ahead of the other teams, they won twenty-four games, lost seven, and tied three, with a winning average of seventy-seven-forty-two. Among the games in which the starting pitcher stayed on the mound until the sixth inning, the team won thirty-nine games, lost nineteen games, and tied four, with a winning average of sixty-seven-twenty-four."

"Why?" The doctor was not hiding his irritation. "What kind of word association is that, anyway? How can you think up anything like that?"

"How do I know? You're the doctor. I am just saying whatever comes to mind."

"All right. 'A hit.' "

"A hit? What kind of a hit? A grounder tunneling through the pitcher's feet? Or a Texas leaguer that drops between the right fielder and the second baseman when both of them back off? Or, maybe a ball that made a hard assault on the third baseman, who couldn't handle it, and it was recorded as a hit by a recorder after some hesitation—although in essence it was an error—because the third baseman had no errors for twenty-nine games in a row?"

"Any kind of hit."

"No, doc. There is no such thing as 'any kind of hit.' A hit could be a ball which hit the highest point of the right-field fence and was bouncing on the ground, while the player went around first base and was tagged just before he slid into second, or it could be a grounder that rolled along the first baseline while the fielders waited and hoped it would become a foul ball only to find it stay a fraction of an inch within fair ground. These two are entirely different from each other, you know?"

"All right, then, it is a liner to the center fielder."

"How about runners?"

"Runners?"

"Look, I have to know whether there were any runners on the diamond. Runners on first and third? How about the out-count? And what about the score? One or two runs difference? Without that knowledge, I can not visualize the kind of fielders' shift the opponent has on the field. If the bases are loaded and the difference in score is three runs, the first and third basemen have to stand close to the foul lines to defend against long hits, while, if the score difference is only one, they have to come forward so that they can aim for a double play. Then, a liner to the center fielder won't be able to bring back the runner on second base to home. On the other hand, if we have runners on second and third with a score difference of three points, the left and right fielders must be close to the foul lines, and the center fielder has to position himself deep in center field. If it's a half-liner, the center fielder has to rush forward fast. Since the second-base runner would have left second base, it would be a close play. Don't think this kind of judgment is easy. If you are too involved in catching a runner at home base, you might end up letting the batter advance to second. It is foolish to allow a tying runner. Wait a minute. Which inning are we talking about? We could let a batter walk intentionally to load the bases. Doc, I can't imagine anything without knowing all these factors. There's no such thing as 'a hit in front of the center fielder.' A hit is a more specific thing. 'Specific!' You understand, doc? All right, so you want me to associate it to something anyway. 'A hit in front of the center fielder, eh?' I distinguish one 'hit in the center fielder' from another 'hit in the center fielder.' And I imagine another 'hit in the center fielder' from the 'hit in the center fielder.' All of these 'hits in front of the center fielders' are connected to each other. Doc, you say that I have an 'insecure feeling.' Can that be true? You know, I feel 'insecure' only when I confront a sidearm southpaw. Oh, I can't get along with them. I went only six for nineteen from them. Two-forty overall. No, I don't dislike them. I rather kinda like them. 'Insecurity is a certain sympathetic antipathy, and an antipathetic sympathy.' A cute remark. If a guy is brainy enough to say something like this, he can be a cleanup in any team. No sweat. It was you who taught me that it was Kierkegaard who said that. In any case, sidearm southpaws tend to have crooked minds somehow, and the balls they pitch are affected by their minds. The balls they pitch are surrounded by some kind of ozone-layer-like thing, and they cause some oxygen-poor conditions along their passages. I think that's why I was swinging at them a little too quickly. But I can't help looking at them. Then I begin to feel funny. Is it 'insecurity?' No? I think you should stand in a batter's box just once and watch a ball come toward you. I think that would help you much more than showing a patient a funny picture or hypnotizing him. The pitcher is an honest animal. All he has will be on the ball he pitches. So the batter looks at it closely. There's nothing as interesting as that in this whole world. It's much more interesting than a novel or a movie. Doc, I am not in a slump. It's just that I can't find the right ball to hit. But why? I wonder. How come I don't have a ball to hit anymore? I wait and wait, but I can't find a ball to hit. I don't know how to describe it, but I just know that they are not the ones I should be hitting. Everything is connected in baseball. Don't cut this connection. One of my uncles who taught me baseball once said, 'If you lose a tie, you are finished.' 'You may not understand yet, but the most important thing in baseball is the tie.' The ace pitcher of our team seems to have lost the tie. *He* is in a terrible slump. Sure he is doing fine in statistics. But that has nothing to do with baseball. I know. Other guys may not understand it, but I do. It's a slump, all right. On the other hand, I am not in a slump, even though I got only three hits out of seventy-six times at bat. I am playing decent baseball games. It's just that I can't find the right balls. Doc, please tell those guys. Those guys who haul balls at me from the pitcher's mounds to throw the balls I can hit. Don't just pitch balls. Tell them to throw balls thinking whether the balls they throw are the balls to be hit. Then they should understand. I am in no slump at all, rather, I am in the best condition I have ever been in since I started playing baseball. I have never felt so good being in the batter's box. When I come out of the batter's box, I am feeling as fresh as if I just had a good night's sleep. I don't even remember what I was doing in the batter's box. As soon as the ball comes near me, I know that it isn't the ball I should be hitting. Then something wonderful happens. It's too bad I don't remember what happens then. In any case, I feel I am totally immersed in baseball. Which part of me is in a slump? Ha! Ha! . . . I'd like to know. Batting average? I don't care. It can't go on like this forever. Yes, Leibniz says so. Yes, Leibniz. I just learned about him. 'In fact, we experience a state from which we do not remember anything, a state during which we do not experience any significant ideas within ourselves. For example, it is close to what we experience when we are in a trance or coma or sleep without a dream. In such a condition, the mind becomes not so different from a monad, a state that doesn't last very long; and since the mind eventually comes out of there, it is after all not much more than a monad.' I am thrilled with the expectation of what might come next. When we know that my mind is not much more than a ball. Ha! Ha! That's why I'm not worried at all. No way!"

Translated by Minoru Mochizuki

THE UNSINKABLE MOLLY BROWN

Tamio Kageyama

BORN IN 1947 IN KANDA, TOKYO, TAMIO KAGEYAMA AT-
TENDED KEIO UNIVERSITY, MAJORING IN LITERATURE, AND
MUSASHINO UNIVERSITY OF THE FINE ARTS, MAJORING IN
DESIGN. IN 1968, WHILE HE WAS A STUDENT, HE MADE HIS
DEBUT AS A TV DRAMA WRITER IN A POPULAR VARIETY
SHOW ON THE NTV NETWORK. IN 1969–70 KAGEYAMA
LIVED IN NEW YORK, WHERE HE WORKED AS A COFFEE-SHOP
SINGER. RETURNING TO JAPAN, HE WORKED FOR THE TBS
NETWORK ON VARIETY AND QUIZ SHOWS, AS A WRITER AND
SOMETIMES AS AN ACTOR. CURRENTLY HE IS A FULL-TIME
NOVELIST.

IN 1986, KAGEYAMA RECEIVED THE SECOND KODANSHA
ESSAY AWARD FOR "ONE FINE MESS/SEKEN WA SLAPSTICK"
("LIFE IS A SLAPSTICK"), PUBLISHED BY MAGAZINE HOUSE,
AND HIS **KOKOU KARANO DASSHUTSU (NARROW ESCAPE)**,
PUBLISHED BY SHINCHO-SHA, WON THE YOSHIKAWA FUJI LIT-
ERARY AWARD FOR NEW WRITERS IN 1989, AS WELL AS THE
FIFTH MOST OUTSTANDING NEW WRITERS AWARD FOR AD-
VENTURE NOVELS. HIS NOVEL **TOOI UMI KARA KITA COO
(COO THAT CAME FROM A FARAWAY SEA)** WON THE NAOKI
AWARD IN 1988. KAGEYAMA'S OTHER WORKS INCLUDE **KO-
ROGARU ISHI NO YOUNI (LIKE A ROLLING STONE), TORA-
BURU BASUTA (TROUBLE BUSTER),** AND **KYUUKA NO TOCHI
(VACATION LAND)**.

The person who started calling her The Unsinkable Molly Brown
was my fellow instructor, Togo. It seems that a long time ago
there was an American movie with that title.

"It was a musical, and since I only saw it on the late-night movie ages ago, I've even forgotten the starring actress's name. But the main character was a woman named Molly Brown who had this striking head of red hair."

There was no doubt about it—she had red hair, too. But it wasn't natural as was the hair of the heroine of the American movie Togo was talking about. It was the kind of hair that middle-aged housewives have: tightly permed and dyed a bright red.

"The English title was *The Unsinkable Molly Brown,* which was originally the name of a ship or something, I think."

Togo had studied in Hawaii for two years during college, so his English was good. And unlike myself, who had climbed the ranks to instructor by taking training courses at this diving school, he had earned a professional open-water instructor's license in Hawaii. I guess for an instructor at a diving school in Japan, he's one of the elite.

"It's the 'unsinkable' part, you know. Makes a perfect nickname for her, don't you think?"

It worked well because the woman's name was Mori, which sounded to us like the "Molly" in Molly Brown. But Togo had another, perfect reason for giving her that nickname; one based on a very special physical characteristic.

Quite literally, she would not sink.

Scuba diving is a pretty demanding sport, but the first step, the diving itself, is not all that tough. Although normally a human body floats on the surface of the water, with a little effort, say by kicking at the water with the legs, it soon sinks below the surface. In short, the density of the human body is such that normally it's just a touch closer to floating than it is to sinking. Of course there are also the "anchors"—those people with a higher body density who will naturally sink, even if they take a deep breath and lie motionless in the water. For scuba diving, they have it easy. Scuba diving, you see, is fundamentally different from swimming because, to begin with, the idea is to sink.

The Unsinkable Molly Brown

Well this Molly Brown had a body type which was the exact opposite of these "anchors." The main reason for this seemed to be related to the fact that her body was covered with a considerable layer of cellulite. To put it simply, the woman was obese.

In the diving school I work at, new students are first divided into classes according to their swimming ability. Although I said that scuba and swimming are different, that's only true after a person is submerged. So we divide the classes in this way because, until the dive itself, we need to have the students swimming and, more importantly, since people who are strong swimmers aren't afraid of the water, they make faster progress. Molly Brown made an impressive showing on her swimming test. When she appeared poolside with what appeared to be over 175 pounds of body crammed into a fluorescent pink one-piece, all of us instructors had a nasty premonition. But she took to the twenty-five-meter pool, if not the way a fish takes to water, then at least the way a sea lion or an elephant seal takes to water. On the way down she did the breaststroke, and on the return, the sidestroke. According to her training card, she was forty-two (we didn't believe it—Togo thought she was forty-five, and I put her at forty-eight), so her speed was nothing to rave about, but she had a good solid stroke. She had probably belonged to a swimming school. Anyway, it seemed she was good in the water. At the time I even felt a certain dignity rising from that enormous body wrapped in pink cloth, a dignity which seemed to frown upon the other new students, all dizzy office girls clinging tenaciously to the edge of the pool shrieking things like, "Huh? Oh boy! I can't swim!"

Naturally, she made it into the top of the three classes, the one which starts with snorkeling practice in the pool. Half of the six students already had some experience snorkeling. I put her in that class because, judging from the way she swam, I thought she would soon get used to using the snorkel and fins.

The trouble started when, mask and fins in place and the snor-

kel in her mouth, she began to practice squatting down in the
1.2-meter section of the pool. For the life of her, once in the
water she couldn't squat. You'd think anybody could bend their
knees and drop their buttocks until they hit the bottom of the
pool, but for her it was an unbelievably difficult operation. She
could somehow manage to get as far as bending her knees. But
when her buttocks dropped to a point just above her knees, her
body would start to rotate forward. A powerful buoyancy seemed
to be pushing her body upward. I tried getting in the water and,
grabbing her shoulders, somehow shoving her toward the bottom. This time her body rotated toward the rear. It seemed like
the buoyancy was coming not just from her body, but was also
being produced by her fat legs, each of which seemed as wide as
my waist. With me clinging to her back, her body turned in the
water as if she were doing a slow rear somersault, and first her
feet, still stuck in the fins, then her thighs, and finally her buttocks
would break the surface of the water. Next thing you know she
was back in the original position, just standing in the pool! The
only danger in it was for me: when her fat body rotated in the
water, I was pinned against the bottom of the pool and almost
drowned.

And that was the birth of The Unsinkable Molly Brown.

"How in the world do you take a bath?" I asked her. "I guess
you float there, too, and never get in up to your shoulders, huh?"

"Don't be so stupid!" Molly Brown shook her broad, brawny
shoulders and looked upset.

"I sink right down to my shoulders, I'll have you know! We have
a Western-style bath, and all the new ones have handles on both
sides of the tub."

I guessed she must grab those handles and force herself down
into the tub. I inadvertently pictured Molly Brown taking a bath
in one of the big pools at some hot spring but hurriedly shook
my head and brushed the image from my mind. Imagine one of
the many blimps flying the skies over Tokyo these days, crash-

landed in the water and floating on the surface with a third of its air leaked out—what a bizarre image!

We managed to temporarily solve the buoyancy problem at the snorkeling stage by having her wear a weight belt loaded with lead ballast. However, in Molly Brown's case buoyancy was produced in all parts of her body, so even with a nine-pound belt wrapped around her hips, she found that getting her balance in the water required quite an effort.

"Why do just my head and legs float?"

She confronted me with this question after dragging herself to the surface, having performed an inverted jackknife at the bottom of the pool, her waist pinned to the bottom while her head and legs rose toward the surface making a V-shape.

"Please practice controlling your body in the water—get your body submerged and then stretch it out horizontally. You should be able to do it by using the power of kicking with the fins. It might take a little practice, though."

I guess it was inevitable. The Unsinkable Molly Brown was soon demoted to the lowest class, the one with people who can hardly swim. This seemed to be quite a blow to her sense of pride.

"I hate having to practice with these dead weights!"

The one who was directly confronted with Molly Brown's dissatisfaction wasn't I, but the head instructor of the C class, Togo. It's the same even at, say, a tennis school: common sense in athletic training demands that the best coaches teach the most inept people.

"At least the dead weights sink. In this school it's the ones who don't sink that need the most training."

Saying this over and over again, Togo had Molly Brown practice maneuvering her body in the water. It was crystal clear to me what was on Togo's mind. At this point things still weren't too bad, because the pool had fresh water and was even warm. Fresh water doesn't create nearly as much buoyancy as salt water, and in warm water it's possible to keep training in just a swimming suit. But the final objective of people who come to learn scuba diving is to dive in the ocean. When that day arrived, Molly Brown would be hopping into an ocean with a lot more buoyancy than the pool, and she would be wearing a wet suit, which produced even more buoyancy than her body had itself. The crash-landed blimp!!

Since the day his class was joined by the woman whom he himself had named The Unsinkable Molly Brown, Togo had somehow developed the strange habit of staring into space and shaking his head violently.

But in spite of all this, myself, Togo, and the other instructors had to admit that she was a real go-getter. For example, even Miss Ehara, the female instructor who was serving as head teacher for the lecture section of this course, had to concede, "If I had been that enthusiastic, I bet I would have made instructor two years sooner than I did." Whether it was lecture or pool practice, Molly Brown was always the first one ready to go. When the previous class had ended, she was already standing by fully outfitted; during the lectures she took a desk in the front row; and in the pool she continued to practice maneuvering her body in the water even during the fifteen-minute rest period before her lesson began.

But in spite of all that effort, it was still a total of ten hours of pool practice, as opposed to the usual five, before Molly Brown, shouldering the scuba gear, advanced to the second stage. In actual number of days, a month and a half had passed since she first enrolled. Since she had finished the three-level lecture course in the usual six hours and passed her written exam with an almost perfect score, this means that her final month commuting to the school had been devoted entirely to teaching herself how to submerge her body in the pool, even just a little, while wearing the snorkel and weight belt, and to move forward in a horizontal position, or even a vertical one. She was a good swimmer and so soon mastered kicking with the fins; her form was good, and she didn't bend her knees or ankles unnecessarily. But her body from the buttocks down poked above the surface of the water no matter what, and as she beat about the surface of the water with those acrylic fins, no student dared to swim near Molly Brown for fear of being kicked in the head.

"Don't worry. When you put the scuba gear on the bottom of the tank will come down to your buttocks and take the buoyancy right out of it."

Togo said this, working to keep Molly Brown from losing her enthusiasm. To tell the truth, I was a little worried that even with the scuba gear on, the buoyancy in her stomach would have her spinning horizontally in the water, but Togo was toying with the idea of placing an order for a custom-made weight belt of a new design which had tiny individual weights attached all over the belt in such a way that balance could easily be achieved.

And so somehow, between Togo's instruction and the efforts of the person involved, the day for The Unsinkable Molly Brown to advance to the second stage arrived. Her classmates from the time she enrolled were long gone, having completed their open-water training and acquired the C-card licensing them to dive in open water, so those witnessing Molly Brown's daring attempt in the five-meter diving pool with full scuba attire were students who had enrolled two terms later than she. At this point, I have no intention of telling you whether or not they enjoyed the experience, but at the very least, they witnessed an event which they can talk about for the rest of their lives. It is, however, also a fact that from the very next day three of those students stopped coming completely. On that day, the figure of Molly Brown appeared poolside in what was unmistakably a complete custom-made wet suit made of five-millimeter-thick pink neoprene with bright green vertical stripes.

"Hey," I said, elbowing Togo in the ribs. "That suit's neoprene, you know. Can you imagine how much that's going to boost Molly Brown's buoyancy?"

"No, I can't," Togo answered. "I'm trying to figure out the surface area of her body to calculate the buoyancy, but the numerical value doesn't come to mind in the units I need."

"Well, what units do come to mind?"

"Tatami,*" Togo said. "An eight-tatami, or maybe twelve-tatami area. I can't estimate the surface area of Molly Brown's body in units other than those."

"Badger balls, that's what it is," I said, and Togo nodded. "I just noticed that Molly Brown's face and that red hairdo make her look just like a badger. And that body, all bundled up, looks like badger balls."

I don't know if up to that point Togo had ever carefully scrutinized the testicles of a badger, but I thought the expression was right on the mark. Wearing a pink wet suit, Molly Brown's body had the look of giant testicles wrapped in a leotard of the same color.

"Bring me the weights," said Togo.

"What about the custom-made thing?"

"That's a measly twelve pounds. It's no match for the buoyancy of that wet suit."

"How many pounds do you want?"

"Who knows? Anyway, take the weights out of the belts over there. We'll attach them to the custom-made belt."

It seemed that Togo had no intention of making The Unsinkable Molly Brown wear a BCD at this stage. A BCD maintains neutral buoyancy while the wearer is diving in the water—simply put, it's a contraption that keeps you floating either under water, like a sunfish in the ocean, or on the surface. At our school we use what's called a "jacket-type" BCD; it's a vestlike thing that's built right into the tank harness. As I've explained, the equipment adds buoyancy, so for The Unsinkable Molly Brown it was com-

*A tatami, used as flooring in most Japanese homes, measures approximately three feet in width and six feet in length.

pletely unnecessary. As a safety precaution we always have students wear one when they dive in the ocean, but since in the five-meter diving pool there was no fear of being pulled away by the tide, and he didn't want to add any more unnecessary buoyancy to her, it's no wonder that Togo reasoned the way he did. At least that's the way I defended Togo when, after the incident in question, the president of the school gave him the tongue-lashing of his life.

Poolside, Molly Brown made a pretty gaudy picture standing at attention while she carried the tank and regulator harness on the back of her pink wet suit. Due to the weight belt, which must have been over thirty-five pounds, her footsteps were heavy, but with a triumphant look on her face she glanced around at the other students, put on the mask, and stuck the mouthpiece in her mouth. Togo, being the instructor in charge, was, of course, already in the pool, floating on the surface in his scuba gear. Togo gave her the "go" sign. She used an entry technique she had mastered through endless practice at the snorkeling level—the "giant stride," a foot-first jump in which the legs are spread wide to provide resistance upon hitting the water. The Unsinkable Molly Brown kicked off from the edge of the pool.

In an instant her vertical descent ended in an ass-first collision with the bottom of the five-meter pool. No matter how you look at it, over thirty-five pounds of weight was just too much. Being the model student that she was, even settled at the bottom of the pool with her body bent and her legs lifted high in her standard V position, she didn't panic. Unable to float, or even stand, with all that weight, she simply motioned to Togo with her index finger. Togo went down head first in a big hurry, and Ehara and I, pulling on masks, were right behind him. At the bottom of the pool we tore off her weight belt and scuba gear, and the three of us escorted her back to the surface. The looks of pure terror on the faces of the other students as they whispered among themselves told me that the reputation of our diving school had plummeted.

The first words out of Molly Brown's mouth as she sat panting by the side of the pool came as a complete surprise, and it was probably thanks to them that we got away with losing only three students.

"When I put on the scuba gear, even I sink! What a relief!" she said.

The screaming school president, blue veins bulging, couldn't bring himself to fire Togo, him being one of the elite with an American professional instructor's license and all, and he got away that night with just a sound scolding.

"But by way of an apology I've decided that the school will present Mrs. Mori with a complete set of scuba gear. Of course, we'll be taking the cost out of your salary over the next twelve months." After the president announced this to Togo, we were free to go.

To cheer up Togo, I decided to take him out for a drink. I ran into Ehara in the locker room and invited her to come along.

"What on earth made Molly Brown want to take up scuba diving?" I said this as I knocked back a glass of beer in a pub in Kabuki-cho.

Togo shook his head. "From now on what do you say we quit using the adjective 'unsinkable' in reference to her. Every time I hear the word I can't help remembering what happened today."

"She was talking about diving in Okinawa," Ehara said.

"What are you talking about?"

"She showed me a map during a lecture session. Some place on the west coast of Okinawa's main island that has a marine station. Uh. . . . Somewhere on the shore opposite Iejima. An area called Naki something-or-other."

"You mean Nakijin? The place near where they had that old Ocean Expo?" I said, being quite the expert on Okinawa.

"That's it! That's the place!"

"But there's nothing special there. She'd be better off crossing over to Iejima, where the facilities are better and diving points are opened up."

"That doesn't seem to be it, though. It's like she's got memories of the place, or something. 'I want to hurry up, get my C-card, and dive right here,' she said and kept pointing to a specific spot in the middle of a lagoon on the map. Then she asked me stuff like 'Have you ever made a dive here?' "

"I wonder what that's all about?"

"Who knows? But I'm positive she said something like 'An important part of my history sank in the ocean here.' Something like that."

With that Ehara emptied her Harper's and soda in a single gulp. Quite a few women divers are heavy drinkers, and it looked like Ehara could be counted among them.

"I smell a love affair in the way she said that," said Togo, finally perking up. He had been drinking straight Perrier, but at last ordered a whiskey and water.

"But think about her age!"

"Hey, age has nothing to do with love," growled Ehara, single and fast approaching her thirties.

"Sure, but don't you think that talking about a love affair that way sounds more like romance for people in their twenties? That's what makes it so strange. After all, Mori isn't an Okinawan name, and when she was still in her twenties Okinawa hadn't been returned to Japan yet. You couldn't get in without a passport."

"But it's still possible, isn't it? Maybe she was a stewardess or something."

"The Unsinkable Molly Brown?!" screamed Togo and I in unison. "Oh, . . . right. Let's cut the 'unsinkable.' "

"But anyway, do people really use the word 'history' when talking about past love affairs?"

"I do," said Ehara.

"Yeah, but you can use it because you're still young. Past forty and saying, 'an important part of my history'! It makes my skin crawl."

"I've got it!" shouted Togo. "It's no love affair! Okinawa, right? We're forgetting something big. People our age think of Okinawa only as a tourist spot or a place to dive, but Okinawa means something completely different to people of Molly Brown's age."

"What do you mean?"

"It's the war! Say Molly Brown's forty-five."

"I think she's forty-eight."

"It doesn't matter. Anyway, what happened in Okinawa right after she was born?"

"Forty-five years ago?"

"Well, say she was a year old. That makes it forty-four years ago."

"Nineteen forty-five, the war!" I said.

"That's right, the battle for Okinawa. The main island was surrounded by the American fleet, and the shells fell like rain. It was in nineteen forty-five that both the troops from the mainland and the Okinawans were on the verge of death."

"Quite a war buff aren't you, Togo?"

"I saw it on a TV documentary. Hey, that's got to be it. The ship that Molly Brown's father was on must have been sunk in the Nakijin sea during the battle for Okinawa. She started scuba diving because she wants to dive in the same water and touch, with her own body, the sea that her father died in. Or, just maybe, she plans to search for the sunken ship."

All worked up, Togo tilted his drink way back.

"That's the only way to explain all that enthusiasm. Now we've got it—the wellspring of Molly Brown's enthusiasm for scuba diving."

It seemed to me that Togo was just trying to make up for his disaster that day by forcing himself to sympathize with her, but Ehara, who was feeling pretty good by now, was with Togo all the way. "I can understand that. That's got to be it. Enthusiasm like hers can only come from something like that. Wow! Molly Brown might just be something special after all."

At this point Togo and Ehara, both pretty damn drunk, started proposing toasts over and over again, and I got left out for being a party-pooper. That was how the night turned out, but since Togo was back to his old self, I thought it wasn't all bad.

From the next pool practice onward, Togo's enthusiasm in coaching Molly Brown was really something to see. He reminded me of Hoshi Ittetsu from the baseball cartoon—in every way the strict, stoic coach. And for her part, Molly Brown seemed to intuit his enthusiasm and redoubled her efforts.

I guess the saying "A clash of enthusiasms is doomed to failure" applies only to the business world, because the situation seemed to work out within the microcosm of the school. Two weeks after the incident in which she sank to the bottom of the pool, The Unsinkable Molly Brown was able to easily maneuver her body under the water. In a student-teacher partnership with Togo, she passed with flying colors the procedure for dealing with an empty air tank, called buddy-breathing, and having completed her pool training in front of everyone, she took part in the two-day/one-night training expedition to the ocean at Izu the next weekend. I didn't go along, so I only heard about it later: it seems that, as expected, the buoyancy of the salt water gave Molly Brown a hard time until Togo got her submerged by outfitting her ankles with ring-shaped weights he had contrived himself. Even taking everything into consideration, I thought that was going just a little overboard. After all, it seems an awful lot like the Chicago or New York Mafia bumping off stool-pigeons by fitting them with concrete loafers before a dip in the river, doesn't it?

And that's how Molly Brown got her C-card and became a full-fledged scuba diver, although she did set an all-time school record by taking eleven weeks to do it.

It was over a month after that Togo asked me if I wanted to go to Okinawa.

"They're redoing the pool next week, so it'll be closed for at least a full three days, and we won't have any classes. If we take a day off before and after the closing, we'll have plenty of time for diving."

Although the cherry blossoms were not even near blossoming here on the main island, down in Okinawa they had long since scattered. But I was interested in going to Okinawa because this was the season when a gigantic fish called a manta ray comes to the Yonara Channel off Ishigaki Island. As soon as I heard that the tour which Togo was inviting me to join included Ehara and one other, it hit me: the goal was not the manta rays of Ishigaki.

"You're planning to make a birdie of it by including The Unsinkable Molly Brown, and dive at Nakijin, aren't you?"

"She begged me to be the dive-master."

"Did you hear the story? Did you check out the war-story thing?"

"You can't directly ask someone something like that. But if we go together we'll figure it all out. That's why I took on everything from putting the tour together to being the dive-master."

Ehara had decided to go for the same reason: to discover what it was that inspired Molly Brown in her scuba diving. In the end I decided to join the tour myself. For just the first two days I would accompany them to Nakijin, and then I'd head off for Ishigaki Island.

Nakijin is a four-hour drive from Naha, but it's got a diving school affiliated with ours, so everything was pretty convenient. It had been a month since I last saw Molly Brown but, as always, her hair was tightly permed and a bright red. Her face, though, had a good tan. When I asked her about it, she said that since she got her C-card she had been diving like mad all over the Izu Peninsula and Hachijo Island.

"But now that I'm finally going to dive at this spot in the ocean, my heart is pounding," said Molly Brown as she sat in the stern of our chartered fishing boat, her hair being teased by the sea breeze.

"Well, your heart may be pounding, but there's really nothing special about this point, you know. It's about twenty meters deep, but they say the visibility isn't very good."

Ehara nodded at this as she zipped up her wet suit.

"Apparently there's some coral, but the glass-bottom tour boats are all over the place. The spot is not meant for diving. Some of the locals told me that there was fighting on the land during the battle for Okinawa, but the American troops controlled the ocean from the very start, so there aren't any sunken ships."

While we were whispering back and forth, a glass-bottom boat filled with middle-aged tourists slowly slid by our fishing boat. Molly Brown had been staring at the land and a group of boulders in the offing, as if lining them up in a triangular surveying technique, and at that instant she shouted. "This is it! Drop the anchor here."

"What's here?" I asked Molly Brown, who was yanking on her scuba gear atop the now stationary fishing boat.

"I was here as a tourist last summer riding in one of those glass-bottom boats. While I was looking at the water from the edge of the boat, the Cartier diamond brooch I bought in Paris dropped into the water. But I'll find that thing, just you wait and see!"

With that The Unsinkable Molly Brown leapt into the water with a giant stride, and I watched in disgust as her ass in the pink wet suit bobbed on the surface.

Translated by James Dorsey

WINE

Mariko Hayashi

MARIKO HAYASHI WAS BORN IN YAMANASHI-KEN IN 1954 AND
WORKED AS A COPYWRITER BEFORE THE PUBLICATION IN
1983 OF RUN RUN WO KATTE OUCHI NI KAEROU (LET'S BUY
'RUN, RUN' AND GO HOME), THE FIRST OF SEVERAL COLLEC-
TIONS OF HER ESSAYS. SHE BECAME A FULL-TIME WRITER IN
1984 WITH THE PUBLICATION OF HER FIRST NOVEL, HOSHI-
KAGE NO STELLA (STARRY STELLA), WHICH WAS NOMINATED
FOR THE NAOKI AWARD. SHE WON THE NAOKI IN 1986 FOR
SAISHUBIN NI MANIAEBA (IF I CAN MAKE THE LAST TRAIN)
AND KYOTO MADE (TO KYOTO), AND SHE HAS ALSO WON THE
FIFTIETH BUNGEI-SHUNJU READERS AWARD.

Our tour guide, Nicole, shrugged her shoulders slightly as she descended the stairs leading to the cellar. I knew that this was something she habitually did when she was feeling self-satisfied. Although it was only our second day in Quebec, I wondered how many times we had already seen her do this. She was a plump, good-natured woman of middle age. Similarly, whenever she was bored by the chateau or neighborhood through which she was guiding us, she showed it plainly on her face. At such times, we felt obligated to keep up a running volley of *très bien*'s.

Suddenly she began to speak in rapid French. Our interpreter, Mrs. Endo, translated it into Japanese that had a slightly odd intonation.

"I'm going to show you Canada's best wine cellar. You rarely see a cellar this fine—even in France."

Oh, wine. Just hearing the word makes me feel tense. Being a free-lance journalist, I think that I have a wider smattering of miscellaneous knowledge than the average woman. But wine is my one weak area. Two years ago I wrote an article about wine for a certain women's magazine. The sommeliers and oenophiles I met at that time thoroughly annoyed me. They were able to recite from memory tediously long names of wines that I wouldn't remember even if I heard them a hundred times, and they spoke in the secret language of vintages. And they had a strange look in their eyes to begin with. After seeing the way they appeared to lick their lips when discussing the better specimens, I vowed never to set foot in the territory of wine again.

But I also hate to be seen as an ignorant child. So I sometimes skim articles about wine before going to restaurants and bars. Naturally, though, I tend to forget everything I've read by the time I reach my destination.

"This is a famous wine cellar," Mrs. Endo said, pushing the wooden door open. "People come from as far away as Montreal to buy wine here. Because the province of Quebec has a direct link with France, this cellar has an extensive collection of wines that you can't get elsewhere."

The moment I set foot in the wine cellar, I was at a loss for words. I had never been in a place so authentic, and I was overwhelmed by the sight. The low brick ceiling extended as far as the eye could see. Small lamps burned here and there in the dim, chilly room. When my eyes became accustomed to the dimness, I could see dull light reflecting from the round bottoms of thousands of bottles. It reminded me of a study lined with foreign books.

Apparently the wine cellar was part of Nicole's standard tour. She guided us into the interior of the cellar with a practiced air.

She suddenly turned around to face me in front of the racks

and asked me in English if I liked wine. Her English pronunciation was as poor as that of most Quebecois.

"I like to drink it, but I don't know that much about it," I replied, in equally halting English. As if he had overheard, a man appeared before us. Tall and bearded, he looked like a scholar. Or at least like someone who worked in a bookstore. Just as I was wondering why it is that men involved with wine so often have a scholarly air, I surprised myself by murmuring, "Maybe I should buy a bottle to take home as a souvenir."

Nicole snapped her fingers happily. She said something in French that I couldn't really understand, but I took it to mean "Just as I expected." The bearded man was called over.

"This lady says she would like you to select a good bottle of wine for her," Mrs. Endo murmured. Holding up one finger, as if to say, "Leave it to me," the man began selecting bottles of wine from a nearby rack.

"He says that he knows Japanese people like white wine and that he would suggest something like this."

Mrs. Endo's finger, the nail painted pink, pointed to the price tag. "Ten dollars: a little over two thousand yen. Is this what you had in mind?"

"No," I answered decisively. At that moment, I was afflicted with a sudden urge to confound these foreigners. They were mocking me with their talk of a two-thousand-yen bottle of wine. Even in Japan I drink wine a bit more expensive than that. I wondered if I looked that young and impoverished.

"Since this is such a good opportunity to do so, I want to try a good wine. I'd like to splurge and spend about ten thousand yen and drink it at the hotel."

"Ten thousand yen? Well." Mrs. Endo, eyes widened, was clearly not being sarcastic. "I live here, and I've never had wine that expensive. You must be rich, Ms. Sone."

"Not at all. But a wine of that price would cost five or six times that much in Japan, so experiencing one here would give me something to remember back in Japan."

Mrs. Endo communicated that to Nicole and the man, who were looking at me dubiously.

"He wants to know what kind of wine you like." I may have imagined it, but I felt that his attitude toward me had become a bit more polite. It was truly regrettable that I couldn't think of the name of any particular wine at that moment.

"Ten thousand yen. A wine of around that price." As I said that I was sure that the man was laughing at me inside. His expression didn't change, however, and he began jingling the keys attached to his belt.

"He says the expensive wines are over here." The racks were in an enclosure shaped like a cask. He unlocked it and beckoned to me. The area inside, which measured about six feet by nine feet, seemed to be walled in with bottles of wine. You could tell at a glance that they were old, because the labels had faded or peeled off altogether. To mask the confusion that had engulfed me, I picked up one of the bottles.

"Oh, you have this one. . . ."

Naturally I had no idea what wine it was. But under the circumstances I felt that I had to say something like that.

Holding a bottle in each hand, he seemed to be asking my opinion. Rather than the labels, I looked at the price tags below them, but I couldn't make them out.

"Forty-five dollars. That's just about right, isn't it?"

At the sound of Mrs. Endo's voice I said, "Yes, yes," over and over.

"This is a great wine. It would cost you the equivalent of . . . ah, let's see . . . eighty thousand yen, even to drink it in a Canadian restaurant."

"Is that right—would it cost that much? Let's all drink a toast with it tonight."

"Great. I'd like to join you," Omura, the photographer, said loudly. He hadn't spoken up to that point.

The man was smiling at us and putting the wine into a box. He was trying to stuff packing in around it, so awkwardly that I couldn't bear to watch.

"Oh, never mind. Will you please tell him that we're going to be drinking it soon, so he can just put it in a paper bag." Before I finished speaking, Mrs. Endo exclaimed "Oh, dear," in a soft but piercing voice. "Ms. Sone, look. What should I do?" She was pointing at the cash register, which was displaying the figure 145. "I mistook the price. I thought something was strange. He kept saying that this wine would cost several hundred thousand yen in Japan, and I kept wondering how something that cost only ten thousand yen could be worth that much. What should I do?"

Mrs. Endo, the wife of a businessman, was only called upon as an interpreter during the busy season. She was showing a surprising lack of sophistication by acting as flustered as if this were her own problem. "It's my fault. I didn't see the number one in front of the price. What should I do? It seems absurd to pay a hundred and forty-five dollars for a bottle of wine."

That scarcely needed to be said. Because I was on a trip, I had decided to buy a bottle of wine in the ten-thousand-yen class, more than I would usually spend. But I had had no intention of spending more than three times that amount.

"What shall I do? Shall I have him exchange it for that two-thousand-yen bottle we were looking at earlier?"

Apparently noticing something odd about the way we were acting, the man stopped wrapping up the wine. He looked at me with his blue-green eyes. At that moment I decided to bear the heavy expense rather than submit to the humiliation of explaining what had happened.

"I can't say I made a mistake about the price. It seems like I'm being given a punishment for showing off, but that's all right. I'll take it."

Wine

Two days later I was on a plane heading back to Tokyo. The box holding the wine was bulkier than I expected; with it and my carry-on bag, my hands were full. I couldn't get it all the way under the seat so it stuck out into the aisle a bit.

"Miss?" A Japanese flight attendant approached me with a smile that was rendered utterly insincere by the cold look in her eyes. "Let me take that paper bag for you."

"No." I shook my head. "This is a very expensive wine. I'm worried about turbulence, so I want to keep it close by." I was trying to put into practice the smattering of knowledge I had: "Hold wine when riding on a plane."

"But it will be in the way of the other passengers, so I'll take it for you," she said, still smiling.

"All right. It won't be a problem if I hold it in my lap, will it?"

With her lips resuming their normal position, she left without saying anything further. I held it like that for a while, but it was tiring. I pulled my bag in front of me with my feet and put the wine on top.

Walking around carrying a bottle of wine was like walking around carrying china. At each hotel and airport along the way, I said in English: "This is a very expensive wine. Be careful, please." I ended up carrying it myself rather than entrust it to a porter. I realized that I had become more neurotic than I would have thought possible. I couldn't bear it—each time the plane shook, I felt as though the wine were emitting a little cry. "I'm being ridiculous," I smiled wryly to myself. I was acting just like those crazy oenophiles—the ones who treat wine as though it were a baby, saying that it breathes. Wasn't I the one who was supposed to have scorned them? Then, the moment I happened to buy some expensive wine, I had gotten all flustered and could think of nothing else.

"Hey, what are you going to do with that wine?" Omura asked from the seat next to mine. I felt guilty that the part of the package I couldn't let go into the aisle was infringing on his leg room, but I didn't mention it. I had asked him to hold the paper bag for me countless times, and each time I had begged his pardon most humbly.

"I just wanted to try a thirty-thousand-yen wine." Naturally I had cancelled the promised wine party at the hotel. I had decided to take the wine back home with me, murmuring over and over to myself, "When I get back to Tokyo I'm going to sell it to someone for a really outrageous price."

"I'll call you if I open it."

"It's also nice to give a party to pay homage to a bottle of wine. You know, with some cheese to go with it."

"I didn't realize. . . . Do you know a lot about wine, Omura?"

"No, just what the average person knows. As it happens, before we went to Canada I was working on a project involving wine."

"I suspected as much." I laughed softly with him.

"The best thing would probably be for you and your boyfriend to drink it together, wouldn't it?" Omura yawned as he spoke, as if he were sleepy.

"That would definitely be a waste. How could a child like him possibly understand wine?"

"What do you mean, a child? He's the same age as I am, isn't he?"

"Is that right? I thought you were older than he is."

I thought of Kunihiko's face, which looks like a child's when he gets angry. Four years my junior, he was a photographer like Omura.

"You're terrible—just because you're attached to him you treat the rest of us as if we were your uncles." Closing his eyes, Omura laughed.

Kunihiko was there to meet me at the airport. Because I had ordered him to be. I had contributed half the money for our used Honda on the condition that he would be the driver. We dropped Omura off along the way and headed to Yoyogi, where I was renting a two-bedroom apartment.

"What did you bring me?" As soon as we were alone together, Kunihiko's tone became flirtatious. He had a mustache, but it had the unintended effect of emphasizing the childishness of his face.

"I got you a book of photographs."

"That's kind of austere. Don't you have anything more exciting?"

"When it was time to leave I didn't have many dollars left, and I ended up buying something boring. I wasn't able to get much of anything for myself, either."

"What do you mean, something boring?"

"A thirty-thousand-yen bottle of wine."

"I've drunk wine worth that much before. Last year when we finished that special edition, the chief editor treated us to some in Roppongi."

"Let me explain something to you. When you buy wine at a restaurant, it costs three times the original price. Furthermore, when it's imported there are other added costs. So how much do you think a thirty-thousand-yen bottle of wine would cost in Japan?"

"I see." Kunihiko gave a whoop of joy. "Let's drink that expensive wine together! To celebrate your homecoming."

"You've got to be kidding." I sniffed. "That would be casting pearls before swine. I'm sure you have no idea of the trouble I went through to bring this wine back here. I'm going to let someone who can really appreciate it drink it."

"You scare me."

I was in a bad mood. Kunihiko was acting as though he wanted to stay over, but I chased him off early, saying I was tired.

"What do you mean? I was looking forward to seeing you." It couldn't quite be taken as a parting shot, but with those words he left, clutching the book and T-shirt I had brought him. Hearing the Honda's engine in the distance, I collapsed on the sofa. I had heard the gossip. A twenty-year-old layout artist had fallen madly in love with Kunihiko. They had probably seen each other con-

stantly while I was away. I hadn't failed to notice the new deco-
ration on the car window. Kunihiko may have put it there deliberately for me to see. Maybe it was just my fatigue and the
sentimentality that accompanies coming home from a trip, but I
was beginning to think that our relationship might be ending.

Still lying down, I looked at the paper bag that was next to the
suitcase and wondered where I should keep the wine. I had
heard that you're supposed to keep it in a cool place where the
temperature is stable, but there was no such place in my apartment. The rainy season had ended while I was in Canada, and
now I could see the midsummer sun through the curtains. I knew
the apartment was probably like a steam bath when I wasn't
there. I had to hurry up and give the wine to someone.

But who? Among my acquaintances, Kishima, an illustrator,
knew the most about wine. More of an artist than an illustrator of
late, Kishima was actually famous. He was also widely reputed to
be a snob. I had heard that he had pet snakes in his huge Japa-
nese-style mansion in the Hongo section of the city and that he
played with them amid his art nouveau furniture. He had a weakness for good food and fine wine and often wrote essays on those
subjects. In fact, I had become acquainted with him after I had
been to pick up a manuscript from him. Kishima would understand the value of this wine and appreciate it more than anyone
else, but I didn't know him well enough to give it to him as a gift.
Besides, a thirty-thousand-yen item that represented the height
of extravagance to me might well seem commonplace to him.
The thought of this rankled me, somehow.

I wanted to use this wine on someone who would really appreciate it. In that sense, Morita seemed to be my only possibility.
He was the assistant editor of a women's magazine that gave me
a lot of work. In fact, this Canadian assignment was the type of
thing that could have easily gone to someone else if it hadn't
been for his strong backing of me. We were fairly close, too, perhaps because we were close in age. A rugby player in his college

days, Morita had a slightly rough way of dealing with people that I found refreshing. If anything, I prefer men who are a little thick-skinned.

"Hi, it's me."

"So, you're back safely."

"I'll come in to the office tomorrow."

"There's no hurry. You can wait until the photos have been developed."

"I brought back some wine."

"Oh, yeah? Is Canadian wine supposed to be good?"

"It's not Canadian. I hadn't known it, but a lot of good French wine is shipped to Quebec."

"That's great."

Morita had a loud voice. And as often seems to be the case with loud-voiced men, he liked to drink. He also loved to teach women things. I had gone with him to countless bars and listened to his lectures.

"Red should be chilled for just thirty minutes. Exactly thirty." So he would order the bartender, tapping on his watch. His greatest happiness was to put on an act of this sort, first becoming a regular customer and then a valued patron who received special treatment.

"Is it Bordeaux or Burgundy?" I could picture his face as his voice came over the receiver. He was probably talking loud deliberately, so the entire editorial department would be able to hear him.

"How should I know? I think it was Chateau something."

"You don't even know that 'Chateau' is part of the name of the really good Bordeaux wines?"

"I'm not the connoisseur you are, Mr. Morita."

"You don't have to be a connoisseur to know that much. Spell the name for me."

"Right now?"

"Yes. Go on."

I put my hand in the paper bag reluctantly. For some reason I felt really angry. Every woman hates to tear open a package that has been wrapped so carefully.

"Let me see. S, A. . . ."

"Wait a minute. I can't understand it like that. Read it correctly, in French."

"I can't. I forgot all my French after college. I studied it as my second foreign language."

"Never mind, then."

The sound of Morita clicking his tongue came clearly over the receiver. He was known for his impatience.

"Okay, then, be sure to bring it tomorrow. Without fail."

He hung up without waiting to hear my response. He had said he could wait for the manuscript, but when it came to something he wanted, it had to be tomorrow.

"What are you talking about? The truth is, you don't know anything," I said aloud. Everyone knew that. Every person with any sense soon realized that although Morita put on a brave front he was actually timid. As a native of rural Kyushu who had come to work at a publishing company, he concentrated all his energy on not being made a fool of. He really did know a lot about music, fashion, new shops, and food. But because he tried to show off his knowledge, the lengths to which he had gone to obtain it soon became obvious to people. The same was true of wine. I had seen this once. Morita had a small card with a table of vintages printed on it. He carried it around with him and was always trying to memorize it.

"Thirty minutes. Chill it for exactly thirty minutes." Those words must have appeared in some magazine as well.

I seemed to have become malicious ever since I had bought the wine. I no longer wanted to give it to Morita. If possible, I thought, I wanted this wine to be drunk by a man who was close to perfect. But was there such a person in my life?

When I woke up it was dark. It was three o'clock in the morning. Unbelievably, I had been asleep on the sofa for more than twelve hours. This was no way to get rid of my jet lag. As I feared, when I started to get up I felt slightly nauseated. It wasn't good that I had had to miss going to the doctor for a while.

About this time last year, I had lost consciousness and been taken to the hospital. They couldn't determine the cause, and I went around to a number of hospitals to have tests. Then the editor of a health magazine told me about the Okamura Clinic on the Ginza. The Okamura Clinic is for rich people, and when I heard the name I knew it wasn't my kind of place. But the editor kindly wrote me a letter of introduction, and I was able to get an appointment with Dr. Okamura himself. When he determined that my blackout had been the result of autonomic ataxia caused by fatigue, I felt admiration for him and understood why he had the reputation he did. I didn't have to become an in-patient; instead I started going to the clinic every ten days. Normally people treated by the head doctor at a clinic slip him tens of thousands of yen in addition to the usual fee as a token of their appreciation, but Dr. Okamura understood that I was a single woman. I had never given him so much as a bottle of whiskey.

I should give the wine to the doctor, I thought. Morita will probably complain a lot, but he's a simple man, so I'll be able to get out of it somehow. Dr. Okamura is a far more appropriate recipient for my wine than Morita.

Not only was he a famous doctor, he was also reputed to be a man of refined tastes. He wrote haiku that were sometimes published in magazines. He was also reputed to be the president of a sumo fan club.

I prettied up the wine. I didn't think the paper bag from Quebec would be appropriate, so I went to a specialty shop and bought some high-quality rice paper. I thought that a ribbon would be overdoing it, so I attached a light green seal.

Wrapping it up in a kerchief, I headed over to the Okamura Clinic on the appointed day. In the three days I had spent taking it easy at home, my jet lag and fatigue had completely disappeared. I had worn jeans the entire time I was in Canada, but today I wore a white linen dress.

My heart raced when I imagined the expression on the doctor's face when he received the wine. He would appreciate its value more than anyone. A lot of his patients were the owners of the Ginza's oldest shops. Surely there would be someone to appreciate it with him.

But I couldn't decide when to give the doctor the wine. There were many other doctors and nurses in the examining room, and I usually wasn't even with him for five minutes.

"You're not having the headaches anymore. Let me check on you again in ten days." With those words, the doctor swiveled around in his chair to face his desk, and the beautiful gray hair on the back of his head faced me. I hadn't had a chance to give him the package that I had left by the door.

I had no choice but to leave it at the reception desk. Naturally, that wasn't the way I would have liked to present it. I had imagined the ripping of the paper and his exclaiming, "Oh, Chateau. . . ." He would certainly have pronounced it correctly. But apparently the doctor and I would not be playing out that scene after all.

"Uh, this is for Dr. Okamura. . . ." As I uttered the words, I realized that I had forgotten something important. My name wasn't on the package. As an emergency measure I decided to tape a piece of paper with my name on it to the package.

"Could you please lend me some tape?"

The receptionist seemed to understand what I was trying to do. Nodding pleasantly, she opened a drawer. But the tape wasn't there.

"It was over there." She got up, and, following her with my eyes, I got a clear view of the area she was referring to. There was a huge pile of packages on the floor. Attached to each was a piece of white paper with bold black letters indicating that it was a midyear present. Absent-mindedly, I, who hadn't engaged in the practice for many years, had completely forgotten about the custom of giving midyear gifts to one's social superiors, and even when the season for such giving was.

"Oh, no," I thought immediately. My wine was definitely not a midyear gift. It was not something that could be reduced to that sort of formality. Besides, who knew what would happen to it once it got mixed up in that huge pile. It would end up sharing a fate with the other, boring gifts, like golf balls, white shirts labeled with the name of the tailor who made them, and imported whiskey. My wine had to be something special that existed only for its own sake. It couldn't possibly be left amid this crowd of other things.

Carrying my package, I started walking briskly.

"Here's the tape!" the woman shouted.

"That's all right. I forgot the card."

The moment the automatic door opened, hot air seemed to come up from the ground and envelop me.

"Now what am I going to do?" In my arms, the wine was gasping for breath too. I could hear it saying that it didn't want to go back to that hot apartment.

"What am I going to do? What am I going to do?"

At almost exactly noon, the Ginza around me seemed to flatten into the background, the way things do in old films. Walking along in my white clothes, I felt ludicrous, as if I myself were a present wandering around in search of a recipient.

Translated by Dawn Lawson

KITCHEN

Banana Yoshimoto

THE SELF-NAMED DAUGHTER OF A MARXIST LITERARY CRITIC, BANANA YOSHIMOTO WON THE KAIEN PRIZE IN 1987 FOR **KITCHEN**, A SIXTY-EIGHT-PAGE NOVELLA THAT BECAME A BEST SELLER AND HAS BEEN MADE INTO A FILM. BORN IN 1964 IN TOKYO, SHE GRADUATED FROM NIHON UNIVERSITY, WHERE SHE MAJORED IN LITERATURE AND ART. HER OTHER WORKS INCLUDE **TUGUMI,** WHICH WON THE YAMAMOTO SHU-GORO PRIZE IN 1988; **WHILE FAST ASLEEP**; **BUBBLE/SANC-TUARY**; **SAD PREDICTION**; AND A COLLECTION OF ESSAYS, **PI-NAPPLIN**. THIS STORY IS AN EXCERPT FROM THE NOVELLA **KITCHEN**.

Kitchens are the places I like best in this world. I'm happy with any kind of kitchen, no matter where it is or what condition it's in. When I'm in a kitchen, a place where I can cook, everything seems fine.

I prefer a functional kitchen that has seen some use, with draw-ers full of clean, dry dish towels and sparkling white tile on the walls and counters. I must admit, though, I have even been at-tracted to a dirty kitchen, where the floor has carrot peels and flecks of onion skins stuck to it and is so grimy that it makes the bottoms of your slippers black. This kind is good if it's really huge.

There stands a hulk of a refrigerator with enough space to store a winter's worth of food. I lean against the shiny door, glance away from the grease-spattered stove and the rusty knives, and gaze out the window at the stars shining far away in the night sky.

It's just me and my kitchen now. Or should I say that I'm all alone? No, I'll comfort myself with the thought that I still have my kitchen.

Sometimes, when I'm really tired, I sit and think about the time when it will be my turn to die, and I always conclude that I want to breathe my last in a kitchen. It might be some freezing cold place I end up in, with no one around, or maybe a nice, warm room with someone holding my hand. Either way, I want to know what is happening to me, and I want to be in a kitchen.

Before the Tanabes took me in, I had been sleeping in the kitchen every night. In my own room, I tossed and turned all night long, and so I kept trying different places in the apartment. One night, I discovered that I felt most comfortable next to the refrigerator.

My name is Sakurai Mikage. Both my parents died young. My grandparents took care of me after that. Just before I entered middle school, my grandfather died. Then my grandmother and I lived together for a long time.

The other day, my grandmother died. I couldn't believe it.

Sometimes, I realize that I used to have a family, a real family, but over time it grew smaller and smaller, until now I'm the only one left. When I think of my life in those terms, everything seems unreal. Time has passed, as it always does, in these rooms where I've grown up, but everyone else is gone. What a shock.

It's just like science fiction. This vast, dark universe.

For three days after the funeral, I was in a daze. I felt so over-whelmed and sad that I didn't even cry much. With the vague feeling of drowsiness that accompanied my sorrow, I dragged my futon into the kitchen and laid it out. I slept with my blanket clutched close, like Linus. The low hum of the refrigerator pro-tected me from lonesome thoughts. There in the kitchen, I slept quite peacefully. The long nights passed and the mornings greeted me.

I wanted to sleep beneath the stars.

I wanted the morning sun to awaken me.

However! That was not how things worked out. This is what happened instead.

I needed to find a new place to live. Grandmother had left me some money, but not enough to pay the rent on our old apartment. Besides, the place was too big for one person. I went to the store and bought a copy of *Apartment Living* magazine. I leafed through it, and I felt like passing out—trillions and billions of apartments, all exactly the same. I couldn't face the thought of moving.

I lost all my energy. I spent so much time lying on my futon in the kitchen that my joints started to ache. Sometimes I would rouse myself long enough to think about moving—or rather all the reasons I couldn't stand to move. The thought of looking for a place, lugging my things from here to there, arranging for the phone to be installed—it was all too much for me.

It was on one such afternoon that I was visited by a miracle. The doorbell rang. I wasn't expecting anyone on that overcast spring afternoon. I had already given up on *Apartment Living* and, at the time, was absorbed in the task of tying up bundles of old magazines—I realized that I couldn't resist moving forever. Still in a T-shirt and pajama bottoms, I rushed out, unlocked the door, and, without hesitating, opened it. (Good thing it wasn't a robber!)

There stood Tanabe Yūichi.

"Thanks for the other day," I said.

Yūichi had helped me out at the funeral. He was a year younger than I. He had told me that he went to the same college as I did, though I was taking time off from school.

"You're welcome," he replied. "Have you found a place to live?"

"I haven't even looked."

He smiled, "I didn't think so."

"Why don't you come in and have a cup of tea?"

"Thanks, but I have to be somewhere soon," he said, smiling. "I just wanted to stop by and let you know that my mother and I have talked it over, and we want you to stay with us for a while."

"Excuse me?" I replied.

"Please come at around seven o'clock tonight. Here are the directions."

"Okay," I said, without really thinking about it, and took the map from him.

"We'll see you then. Mother and I are both looking forward to having you over, Mikage."

I was not used to seeing someone with such a radiant smile and intense eyes in our front hall, but I looked straight at him. I also hadn't expected him to call me by my first name like that, as if we knew each other.

"Thank you. I'll be there," I answered. I suppose that I should have resisted this temptation, but I felt that I could trust him. He was so "cool," so right. But that's how it is, when everything looks dark, and temptation knocks. I saw only one choice—to take that bright, safe-looking path that he offered.

Yūichi smiled again, said good-bye, and went on his way.

Until Grandmother's funeral, I hardly knew him at all. He showed up on the day of the service and really gave the impression of being one of Grandmother's admirers. His hands trembled when he went up to light a stick of incense. He closed his eyes, already red and puffy from crying. When he opened them and saw her picture there, tears streamed down his cheeks.

Seeing this, I was convinced my feelings for Grandmother lacked the same kind of depth. That was how full of sorrow he appeared.

Still wiping his face with a handkerchief, Yūichi said, "Please, let me help you," and so I had him help out.

Tanabe Yūichi.

It took me a while to remember when exactly Grandmother had mentioned his name. I felt confused.

Yūichi, I then remembered, worked part-time at a florist where Grandmother used to shop. She would often come home with stories about a nice young fellow named Yūichi, and what he had said or done. Grandmother loved cut flowers and always kept a vase of them in our kitchen. She would visit the florist once or twice a week. Actually, I think that Yūichi might have come to our apartment to deliver a potted plant once. I remember him walking along behind Grandmother.

Yūichi was a lanky, good-looking guy. I didn't know anything about his background, but whenever I saw him at the florist, he would be working very hard. Even after I had met him a few times, my impression that he was somehow cool and distant did not change. Although Yūichi was very attentive and sweet when he was talking with other people, he seemed to be living apart. That was all I knew about him. He was a stranger to me.

That evening, it rained. I walked along, map in hand, through the hazy spring darkness, enveloped in the warm rain.

The apartment building where the Tanabes lived was on the opposite side of the park from our place. Once in the park, I felt nearly suffocated by the heady fragrance of the trees. I splashed through the puddles along the pathway, iridescent from the rain.

In all honesty, I was only going to the Tanabes because they had invited me. I had nothing, absolutely nothing, else in mind.

Their apartment turned out to be way up on the tenth floor of a tall apartment building. I gazed up from the street below and imagined how beautiful the view must be at night.

I took the elevator up to the tenth floor. My footsteps echoed through the still hallway. I rang the doorbell and Yūichi came running to open the door.

He welcomed me and showed me into the living room.

It was a truly unusual place. My eyes went immediately to the gigantic sofa, smack in the middle of the room. With its back to the china cabinet that separated the living room and the kitchen, the sofa stood in solitary splendor, no rug beneath it, no table before it.

It was a very grand piece of furniture, upholstered in a chic beige, like something you'd see in an advertisement in a glossy magazine, with a whole family sitting on it and watching TV and a dog too big for any Japanese home lying on the floor next to it.

By the windows that looked out onto the balcony grew a jungle of potted plants. I noticed that there were flowers all over the place. Vases of cut flowers graced every surface.

"My mother's at work now, but she'll be back soon. Why don't you look around a little while we wait? I'll give you a tour," he said, shaking some tea leaves into a pot. "What room do you like to judge people by?"

"Judge what?" I asked, settling back into the sofa.

"Our taste and the character of the house. Haven't you heard that? You know, that you can really tell a lot about someone once you've seen their bathroom, or whatever," he said, smiling faintly. He was very low-key.

"The kitchen," I said.

"Please. Look anywhere you'd like."

He stood in the kitchen making tea, so I walked around him and began my inspection.

The handsome mat on the wood floor, Yūichi's well-made slippers. A small assortment of well seasoned kitchen utensils hung from hooks on the wall. They had a Silverstone frying pan and a German vegetable peeler just like ours. Grandmother, always happy to do things the easiest way, loved the peeler because it was so much simpler to use than a regular knife.

Beneath the glow of a small fluorescent lamp, drinking glasses sparkled and dishes waited for their turn to appear on the table.

I noticed that none of the dishes matched, but they were all extraordinarily fine pieces, so it didn't matter. I felt pleased that they had special things, like big noodle bowls, casserole dishes, giant serving platters, and beer steins with lids. The refrigerator—Yūichi told me I could peek inside—was clean and neatly arranged, without a single plastic container of moldy leftovers.

I approved of everything that I saw. It was a fine kitchen. It took only one look for me to love that kitchen.

I went back and sat on the sofa. Yūichi brought out the tea.

I felt an overwhelming sense of desolation, sitting there in a strange house, with a person I barely knew.

I glanced up toward the window, only to see my reflection floating where the rain-streaked lights of the city blurred into the darkness. I found it amazing to think that I could go anywhere and do anything I wanted, since I no longer had any close family.

Recently, for the first time, I had seen with my own eyes, and felt with my own hands, the vastness of the world and the depth of the darkness. I realized the boundless fascination and sadness of that. I recognized that I had been looking at life with one eye closed.

"Why did you ask me over?" I inquired.

"I thought that you might be having a hard time," he said, with a look of concern in his eyes. "Plus, your grandma was such a wonderful lady. And we have all this space. You have to move out of there, don't you?"

"Yeah, though the landlord's really nice—he's letting me put off the move for a while longer."

"So you can stay here," he said, as if it were the most natural thing in the world.

He was neither nonchalant nor too enthusiastic in his attitude toward me, for which I was grateful. Something about Yūichi moved me tremendously. I felt tears well up inside. Just at that moment, the front door rattled open, and an incredibly beautiful woman rushed in, out of breath.

Surprised, I stared wide-eyed at her. She didn't look young, but she was very charming. Judging from her heavy make-up and unconventional clothes, I immediately guessed that she was some kind of hostess or entertainer.

"This is Sakurai Mikage," Yūichi introduced me.

Still trying to catch her breath, the woman greeted me with a smile and a husky hello.

"I'm Eriko, Yūichi's mother."

I couldn't stop myself from staring. She was not what I had expected. Her long, flowing hair, the shine in her big, almond-shaped eyes, her full lips, her slender, sharp nose—plus that brilliant light, like a visible flicker of life force, emanating from her entire being. I'd never seen anyone like her. I finally realized that I was being a little rude, just sitting there gawking at her, and I managed to say politely, "Nice to meet you."

"We can start getting to know each other tomorrow, okay?" she said sweetly to me, and then turned to Yūichi and explained hurriedly, "Sorry, Yūichi, I've got to rush back to work. The only reason I was able to pop in is that I told them I was going to the bathroom and snuck out. I'll have some free time tomorrow. Be sure to have Mikage stay over so I can see her in the morning."

She turned, in her red dress, and ran back over to the front door.

"Okay, I'll drive you," Yūichi said.

"Thanks for taking time out from work to come see me," I said.

"No problem. I really hadn't expected we'd be so busy today. I hate to have to dash off and leave you like this. See you in the morning!"

She slipped into her high heels and left. Yūichi, trotting along behind her, paused long enough to say, "You want to watch TV or something while I'm gone?" and then vanished.

Upon closer examination, Eriko did turn out to have her share of wrinkles, and some of her teeth were slightly crooked. She was a real person, after all. Still, she had blown me away completely. I couldn't wait to see her again. In my heart, a warm glow remained, like an afterimage. This, I thought, is what you call charm. I felt that I had seen that word come alive before my very eyes. It was a revelation, like when Helen first understood the connection between the liquid that flowed over her hands and the word "water." I'm not exaggerating. That's how surprising the encounter was for me.

I heard Yūichi coming down the hall, his car keys jangling.

"If she could only get away for ten minutes, she should have just called, don't you think?" he said, slipping his shoes off in the entrance way.

"You're right." I didn't get up.

"Mikage, my mother's pretty wild, huh?"

"Yeah. I think she's really beautiful."

"She should be," he smiled. He came into the living room and plunked himself down on the floor right in front of me. "She's had plastic surgery."

"Oh, yeah?" I said, pretending not to be surprised. "So that's why you two don't look alike."

"Right. And that's not all. Could you tell?" he continued, taking obvious pleasure in our exchange. "She's a man."

This time I couldn't fake it. My jaw dropped, and I stared at Yūichi, in total shock. I'll just sit here until he tells me that he's only kidding. Her every move, the way she handled herself, those slender fingers. . . . I imagined her beautiful face and held my breath in anticipation, but Yūichi just sat there grinning, making no attempt to tell me otherwise.

"But, but . . ." I stammered. "You told me she was your mother."

"Well, I can't exactly call someone like that my father," he replied calmly. He was absolutely right. I couldn't disagree with him there.

"Well, where did she get the name Eriko?"

"She made it up. Her real name is Yūji."

All I could see was a vast whiteness. And then, finally, I felt ready to hear more, so I asked, "So who had you?"

"Eriko used to be totally male a long time ago," he answered. "When my father was pretty young, he got married. His wife was my real mother."

"What was she like?" It boggled the imagination.

"She died when I was little, so I don't remember her at all, but I have a picture of her. Want to see it?"

I nodded. He reached over, grabbed the handle of his brief-case, and slid it across the floor to where he was sitting. He took a photograph out of his wallet and handed it to me.

There was nothing special about her. She had short hair and a button nose. You couldn't tell how old she was, but she left an odd impression on me. I was sitting there quietly, looking at the photo, when Yūichi said, "She's pretty weird, huh?"

I didn't know how to respond to that, so I just laughed.

"When she was little, Eriko was taken in by the parents of this woman in the photo—I'm not sure why—but, anyway, they grew up together. When he was a male, he was very good-looking and popular with the girls, so I'm not sure why he chose this weird-looking one." He grinned and looked down at the picture. "He was so attached to my mother that he dropped everything and eloped with her."

I listened quietly.

"After my mother died—I was still pretty little when that hap-pened—Eriko quit her job and tried to figure out what to do with the rest of her life. I guess she decided to become a woman. She told me that she thought she'd probably never fall in love with anyone ever again. Apparently, she was a very quiet type before she became female. She wasn't content to leave things only half-way done, so she went out and had surgery on her face and everything. With whatever money she had left, she bought a bar in town, and raised me. A single mother, as it were."

He laughed.

"What an amazing life," I said.

"Hey, she's still alive, you know," Yūichi retorted.

Could I trust these two? What would he tell me next? The more I learned about them, the more confused I felt. I did, however, trust that kitchen. Another thing was that this mother and son had one thing in common, though they didn't look alike. They both resembled statues of some god or Buddha when they smiled. I liked that. I liked that very much.

"I won't be here tomorrow morning, but feel free to use whatever you'd like," Yūichi said sleepily, his arms loaded with blankets and a nightgown for me. He took me around and showed me how to use the shower and where they kept the towels and things.

After having heard Eriko's life story (unbelievable!), I felt kind of stunned, so I just sat with Yūichi and watched TV. We talked about the florist and my grandma for a long time, and it was one o'clock in the morning before we knew it. That sofa was quite comfortable. It was so soft and roomy and deep that I never wanted to get up.

"You know what I bet?" I ventured. "That your mom was in a furniture store one day and just happened to sit down on this one, and she couldn't walk away from it. She just had to buy it."

"Good guess," he said. "It's the sort of inspiration that she thrives on. What's amazing about her is that she has the strength to carry through with her ideas. It's pretty impressive."

"For sure," I agreed.

"But now the sofa is all yours, for a while, anyway. It's your bed," he said. "I'm happy that we can put it to some good use."

"Yūichi," I said softly, "is it really okay for me to sleep here?"

"Of course," he replied without hesitation.

"I'm very grateful," I said.

Yūichi showed me around the apartment a little more. Then he said goodnight and went to his room.

I felt sleepy.

I stood in their shower and let the hot water flow over me and wash away my fatigue. For the first time in a long while, I wondered about what exactly I was doing with my life.

I changed into the nightgown Yūichi had lent me, and stepped out into the silent living room. I padded barefoot across the wood floor to the kitchen and looked in again. I still liked it.

Then I made my way back to the sofa, my bed for the night, and turned off the light.

Next to the window, the plants breathed quietly, illuminated by the dazzling lights of the city far below. The rain had stopped and the city lights shone brightly through the clear, damp air.

I pulled the blanket tight up around me and smiled at the thought that I was sleeping near a kitchen again. I didn't feel lonely tonight, though. I suppose I had been waiting for a bed where I could forget, if only briefly, all that had been and all that was to come. I didn't want someone in the same bed with me. That would have just made me feel desolate. This was perfect: there was a kitchen, lots of green plants, and another person under the same roof. And so quiet. It was perfect.

I slept peacefully.

The sound of running water woke me up. The room was bright with sunlight. Still half-asleep, I sat up, only to see "Eriko" standing there in the kitchen. She had on a less flashy outfit than the night before, but when she turned to say good morning, her face looked all the more exceptional in the morning light. I felt a bit more awake.

I pushed the covers away and said, "Good morning."

Eriko opened the refrigerator, looked in, and then turned back to me with a dissatisfied expression on her face. "Usually, I'm still asleep at this hour, but I felt really hungry, so I got up. But, look at this, there's nothing to eat. Maybe I'll something delivered. Do you want anything?"

I got out of bed and offered, "Why don't I make something?"

"Really?" she replied eagerly, but then added with a note of hesitation, "You look too sleepy to be cutting up things with a sharp knife."

"I'm fine."

The living room felt like a sun room, with all the light streaming in. Outside the window you could see the perfectly blue sky spreading out forever.

I appreciated being back in the kitchen so much that I felt wide awake and ready to go. Suddenly, I remembered that Eriko was male.

Seized by this thought, I swung around to look at her. An overwhelming sense of déjà vu swept over me.

There was something so familiar about her at that moment. She had curled up on some cushions on the floor. She lay there, basking in the brilliant morning sun and watching TV in that dusty room, redolent of wood.

With great relish, Eriko ate the egg and rice soup and the cucumber salad I had made. It was a sunny spring day, and we could hear the voices of children running about on the playground below.

The plants and blossoms by the window shone a fresh green in the gentle rays of the sun. In the faint blue of the sky on the horizon, light clouds floated by. It was a warm, lazy day.

It was all very strange, sitting there, eating a late breakfast with a perfect stranger. Even the morning before, I would never have guessed that I would be here.

They didn't have a table, so we put all the plates and bowls on the floor. Sunlight shone through a glass of cold tea, making a green pattern of waves on the floor.

"Yūichi has told me several times," she began suddenly, looking at me intently, "that you remind him of our old Non-chan."

"Who's Non-chan?"

"Our puppy."

"Oh." A puppy?!

"Everything about you—your eyes, your hair, just everything. When we first met last night, I really wanted to laugh."

"Is that so?" I hoped Non-chan wasn't—Non-chan couldn't have been—a Saint Bernard or some dog like that.

"When Non-chan died, Yūichi didn't eat for a week, he was so upset. So he must feel something really special for you—whether or not it's romantic love, I don't know." She giggled.

"I feel flattered," I said.

"He told me that your grandma was awfully kind to him."

"Yes, she was very fond of Yūichi."

"I was working the whole time Yūichi was growing up, so he's not a perfect child."

"Not perfect?" I smiled.

"Yes," she insisted in a very motherly way, "he's messed up emotionally and has a hard time getting close to people. I know that he's not all he should be, but he's a sweet boy. At least I succeeded in that. He's a very nice boy."

"Yes, he is."

"You're a nice girl, too."

She—he—grinned at me. She reminded me a little of the timid, smiling faces of gay men in New York that I'd seen on TV, only she was much stronger. A strength of character emanated from very deep inside her, like a shining light; it had made her what she was. I felt certain that no one could have changed that— not her dead wife, or son, or even Eriko herself. She knew only too well the quiet loneliness that comes from being this way.

She swallowed a bite of the cucumber salad and said, "I know a lot of people say things that they don't really mean, but I'm not like that. We want you to stay with us as long as you'd like, okay? You're a sweet girl, and I'm very glad you're here. It's rough not to have someplace to go when you're in so much pain. Think of this as your home." She spoke insistently and looked me straight in the eyes.

"I am prepared to pay you rent," I blurted out, my voice shaking. "Please let me stay here until I've found a new apartment."

"Don't you worry about money. Just make me some of that soup of yours once in a while, okay? Yours tastes a lot better than Yūichi's anyway," she said brightly.

I had felt very uneasy about living alone with an elderly person. The more energetic Grandmother was, the more anxious I would feel. When we were actually together, we had a good time and I didn't worry, but now that I look back on those days, I realize that, down deep, I felt some trepidation.

I had always been afraid—you know, of Grandmother dying.

Whenever I returned home, Grandmother would be watching TV and would come out from the tatami room to say hello. I always brought home two pieces of cake from the bakery when I was late. Grandmother would hardly ever get angry, even if I stayed out until morning. She was a very liberal grandmother.

It was our time together before bed. Sometimes, we'd have coffee with our cake; at other times, green tea. We'd watch some TV.

For as long as I can remember, Grandmother's room never changed. We would sit there and chat about people we knew, gossip about this movie star and that singer, and talk about things that had happened that day. I think that Yūichi was sometimes the topic of our conversations, too.

No matter how madly in love I was, no matter how silly drunk I was, I always had her, my only family, on my mind.

The terrifying silence that lay in wait in the corner of every room, that came pressing in on me. . . . No matter how happy our life together seemed, I knew, even when I was quite small, that there was a gap that could never be filled, a space. No one needed to tell me that.

I think Yūichi felt the same way.

When was it that I discovered that the one thing I could do was to provide my own light on this dark path? My grandmother raised me lovingly, but I always felt alone.

Inevitably, we all scatter in the dark void of time and fade away.

I walked through life completely aware of this reality. Perhaps it was only natural that Yūichi reacted to me the way he did.

And so my life at the Tanabes' began. After I decided to take it easy for the rest of April, daily life became much more bearable. It was like paradise, in fact. I continued to do my part-time job, but I spent the rest of the time cleaning house, watching TV, and baking cakes, just like a housewife. I felt happy that light and air were finally coming back into my soul.

Yūichi was at school or work during the day, and Eriko went to her club every night, so we were rarely all home at the same time. I felt strange sleeping in such an open space, plus, I had to keep going back to the old apartment to pack up, and so I found this new life tiring at first. Before long, though, I became accustomed to it.

I loved the Tanabes' sofa as much as I did their kitchen. I thoroughly enjoyed sleeping on it. Each night, before I fell into a deep sleep, I would sense the city glowing outside the curtains and hear the plants and flowers breathing there by the window. I had everything I wanted and was happy.

I've always been that way. Once I get used to a situation, I don't like to think of change, even if I'm near the edge. I thanked the gods (if there are such things) that someone came and gave me that warm, comfortable bed just then, without my even asking. I would have just sat there, rotting, otherwise.

Each time I went back to the old apartment, I was shocked. It had become a stranger to me since I moved out.

One day, I returned to the old apartment to pack up some

boxes. I opened the door and immediately felt how still and dark it was. Nothing breathed there. All of those old, familiar things seemed suddenly cold and alien. I felt as though I were a guest in someone else's house and that I should tiptoe in, so as not to disturb anyone. Grandmother had died, and time had died there, too. It was undeniable. There was nothing else to do, nothing but to move out. . . . I found myself humming a tune as I wiped down the refrigerator.

Then the phone rang.

I picked up the phone, thinking that it might be Shūtarō, and it was. Shūtarō was . . . my old boyfriend. We broke up around the time Grandmother got really bad.

"Hello, Mikage?" It was great to hear his voice again. It made me want to cry.

"It's been a long time," I said cheerfully, casually, as if it were mere coincidence that we hadn't met. This was some kind of sickness with me, not just a matter of pride or something.

"Yeah. I'd been asking around about you at school, 'cause I never saw you there, and somebody told me that your grandma had died. I just couldn't believe it. It must've been awful for you."

"Yeah, so I've been sort of tied up."

"Can I see you?"

"Sure."

As we were deciding about the time and place, I glanced out the window. The sky was a leaden gray. I could see banks of clouds being whipped along by the wind. So what's so sad anyway? There's nothing sad out there.

Shūtarō loved parks. He liked any place with trees, wide-open spaces, the great outdoors. Even at school, he would hang out in the courtyard or on a bench by the playing fields. Everyone knew that if you wanted to find Shūtarō, you should look for him outdoors. He even said that he wanted to do some kind of work with plants after he graduated.

I always seem to get hooked up with these men who like plants.

We were the perfect couple in those days, when life was normal for me (Shūtarō is always normal and happy). Because he liked the outdoors so much, we would usually arrange to meet at a park somewhere, even in the middle of the winter. I felt awful because I was always late and he had to sit out in the cold waiting for me, and so as a compromise this time we decided to make our meeting place a really big café right next to the park.

That day, Shūtarō sat at a table on the park side of the café. He was gazing out the window when I got there. From the plate-glass window you could see the trees swaying in the wind against the overcast sky. Dodging several waitresses who were bustling back and forth, I made my way over to his table. He looked up and smiled.

I sat down across from him and said, "It kind of looks like rain."

"No, I bet it'll clear up," he answered. "That's pretty funny. We haven't seen each other for weeks and we're sitting here talking about the weather."

His smiling face put me at ease. It was nice to have afternoon tea with someone so familiar. I knew a lot about Shūtarō. I knew that he snored and thrashed about in bed, and that he put tons of milk and sugar in his coffee. I knew that ridiculously earnest look he got on his face when he was looking at himself in the mirror and trying to straighten his wavy hair with the blow dryer. That afternoon, if we had still been going together, I'm sure I would have been upset at how bad my right fingernails looked from cleaning the refrigerator.

"Hey, is it true?" he said abruptly, breaking off our chatter. "I hear that you're staying at Tanabe's place."

Oh, my gosh. I was so surprised that I let my tea cup tip. Tea slopped over onto the saucer. Shūtarō's eyes widened.

"Everybody at school's talking about it. You mean you really didn't know? Unbelievable," he said with a smile.

"Slow down! You're way ahead of me. What kind of rumors are going around?" I asked.

"That Tanabe's girlfriend—I mean his old girlfriend—they were in the cafeteria and she slapped him."

"Because of me?"

"I guess so. Well, you guys are pretty tight, aren't you? That's what I heard."

"What? Who made that one up?" I said.

"But you're living together, right?"

"I'm living with Yūichi's mother and Yūichi." (I didn't have to tell him all the details about the "mother.")

"What!? You're putting me on!" he exclaimed loudly. I used to love the fact that he was so open and lively, but that day I just hoped that people weren't staring at us. Shūtarō was so brash.

"I've heard that Tanabe's kind of different," he said.

"I wouldn't really know," I said. "I hardly ever see him, and we rarely talk. He just took me in like a puppy. I doubt that he feels one way or the other about me. Plus, I hardly know anything about him. And, no, I wasn't even aware that Yūichi was having trouble with his girlfriend. I guess I'm pretty out of it."

"Well, I never thought you really understood what it means to be going together or to be in love or whatever," Shūtarō said. "But anyhow, it seems like you're doing okay. How long can you stay there?"

"I have no idea."

"Well maybe you'd better get an idea," he laughed.

"Yes, sir, I'll try," I replied.

After we left the café, we took a path through the park. I could see the Tanabes' apartment through the trees.

"That's where I'm living now," I told Shūtarō and pointed out the apartment.

"What a great place! Wow, it's right on the park. If I lived there, I'd get up at five o'clock every morning and take a long walk." He smiled.

He was very tall, so I always had to look up at him when we talked. If I had still been with him when Grandma died, I bet, I just bet, that he would have made me find a new apartment right away and probably dragged me over to school too. I glanced over at his profile and considered what life might have been like.

I loved his wholesome approach to life. I adored that about him. And when I was with him I felt disgusted that I was not more like him. Shūtarō was the eldest son of a big family. He possessed a certain brightness, a glow, from having grown up in a home like that, and it made me feel warm inside. I just couldn't. . . . What I needed was the Tanabes' strange kind of brightness and calm but, somehow, I didn't think that Shūtarō would understand that. I suppose I really didn't need to tell him. It was a constant refrain when the two of us were together. I always ended up feeling sad about who I was.

"I'll be seeing you around."

I needed to know, so I asked him with my eyes. Do you still have a place in your heart for me?

He smiled and said, "You take care of yourself." I could see a look of concern in his eyes, but that was it.

"Yes, sir, I'll try," I answered. I waved good-bye and turned to go. The feeling fades away and vanishes in some distant, boundless place.

Translated by Ann Sherif

ABOUT THE TRANSLATORS

Nina Cornyetz received her Ph.D. in Japanese literature from Columbia University. Dr. Cornyetz has translated two novellas by Izumi Kyoka and has published criticism of Masahiko Shimada's work in the *Shincho* literary magazine.

James Dorsey was originally a karate enthusiast, whose five years in Japan turned him into an all-round Japanophile. With interests in modern Japanese literature and literary cricitism, he is currently working toward a Ph.D. at the University of Washington in Seattle.

Joseph Farrar grew up in New London, Connecticut, and graduated from Amherst College in 1979. A Fullbright scholar in 1984–85, he worked for several years as a translator in Tokyo. He lives in New York with his wife, Chiho, and is currently at work on a collection of stories.

Kevin Flanagan lived and taught in Japan for six years. He has a Ph.D. in psychology and practices in Tucson, Arizona.

About the Translators

David Hanna was born in Terre Haute, Indiana, and now lives in Brooklyn, New York. He has had many years of experience in translation of business, technical, and legal material both in Japan and the United States and was very happy to try his hand at a literary piece.

Dawn Lawson received her M.A. in Japanese literature from Harvard University. She has translated *Selected Writings of Nagisa Oshima,* forthcoming from M.I.T. Press. Ms. Lawson lives in New York.

Mauricio Lorence lives in Brooklyn, New York, and is an Assistant Professor of Japanese Language and Culture at Sacred Heart University in Fairfield, Connecticut.

Minoru Mochizuki has lived in the U.S. since 1968 when he attended the University of Minnesota as a graduate student on a Fulbright Scholarship. Mr. Mochizuki works in midtown Manhattan as a bilingual specialist and resides in Port Washington, New York.

Tamotsu Omi was born in Okinawa and lives in Tokyo, where he is an Assistant Director for Telecom Japan TV.

Constance Prener learned Japanese in Japan and did graduate work in Japanese language and literature at the University of Pennsylvania. In addition to her translating work, she is a harpsichordist and performs with various early-music ensembles.

Hiroaki Sato, a resident of New York City since 1968, has published twelve books of Japanese poems in English translation. *From the Country of Eight Islands: An Anthology of Japanese Poetry,* his collaboration with Burton Watson, won the P.E.N. translation prize for poetry in 1982.

About the Translators

Ann Sherif received her Ph.D. in Japanese literature from the University of Michigan. She teaches at Case Western Reserve University and lives in Cleveland.

William J. Tyler has had his *The Bodhisattva,* a critical study and translation of *Fugen,* a novel by Ishikawa Jun, published by Columbia University Press. Other translations include *The Psychological World of Natsume Soseki* and short stories by Ishikawa Jun and Kajii Motojiro. Dr. Tyler lives in Philadelphia.